Cullowhee Baptist Church

NOVEMBER 17 – 190TH YEAR ANNIVERSARY

1821 - 2011

A PLACE OF GRACE AND PEACE

First Edition 2011

Cover: c. 1928—view from Buzzard's Roost, comprising what then was the entire campus of Cullowhee State Normal School. Seen here in the background are the old Cullowhee Baptist Church; Madison Building; old heating plant; Davies Home; the Music & Art Building; Joyner Building; part of the Moore Dormitory in progress, with the overlay of the current Cullowhee Baptist Church.

Layout: Amy Ammons Garza

PUBLISHER
Catch the Spirit of Appalachia, Inc.
Imprint of Ammons Communications
SAN NO. 8 5 1 – 0 8 8 1
29 Regal Avenue • Sylva, North Carolina 28779
Phone/fax: (828) 631-4587

Library of Congress Control Number: 2011941419

ISBN: 978-0-9837382-2-0

This work compiled with assistance from

Cullowhee Baptist Church History Committee and Members
Barbara Dooley, Etheree Chancellor,
John Bell, Amy Ammons Garza,
Dianne Yount, Mary Lou Millwood, Pam Hill,
and other members of the church as listed within the book

With special assistance from WCU Graduate Student Nicole Jarosinski

Edited by Dianne Yount

Catch the Spirit of Appalachia, Inc.
WESTERN NORTH CAROLINA

Above: Up-close view of the church.
This fifth church building was erected in 1918 on land destined to become the campus of Western Carolina University.
Photo taken sometime between 1918 and 1930.

Below: View of the back of our current Cullowhee Baptist Church.
Photo taken Dec 6, 1944. (Note the hay stacks in the foreground.)

Contents

A Message From Our Pastors

The Reverend Dr. Jeffrey & Reverend Tonya Vickery

Cullowhee Baptist Church is an amazing congregation, not simply because of its 190-year history but because the people here have joined together in God's journey of grace and peace .

The Christian life has been characterized as a journey. We are always on "the Way" with Christ in the midst of God's world. For this congregation we know as Cullowhee Baptist Church, it has been a long "Way," full of ministry and mission with still more to be done. Imagine, then, Cullowhee Baptist Church standing on a trail in the mountains. One direction down the trail shows the way we have come in order to be where we are. The other direction shows where we are going next as we continue along the trail. The place where we are standing now is the only place where we can be obedient to God. So as we gather to celebrate the 190-year journey of Cullowhee Baptist Church, we will look back and look ahead and celebrate what we are doing today.

We have had the privilege of being pastors to this congregation for nearly 10 years. The ability for Cullowhee Baptist to respond with generosity, to step out on mission, and to join together for ministry has grown year after year. Rather than repeat our own individual stories from our time here, we want you to see the congregation as it is today.

Cullowhee Baptist gives worship a central place in the life of the church. Our most significant time together as a family of faith in Jesus Christ is on Sundays as we gather for worship. Every Sunday, without fail, church members sit alongside guests who have joined us from the community or university as we sing, pray, listen, and share in the worship of God. Our lectionary-based worship follows the liturgical year, leading us to reflect upon our place in the life of Jesus Christ. Monthly we share in the celebration of communion that unites us with one another in Christ. Various members of the church lead in prayers and scripture readings, children's sermons and singing. Worship is never for us a matter of entertainment, but of honoring the God who both created and saved us. It is the heart of our confession as Christians living in our world trying to be obedient to God's purpose in this place.

Cullowhee Baptist is inter-generational. One of the joys of Cullowhee Baptist is the ability we have to know one another by face and name and family. On a typical Sunday in worship, we have 90-years-olds worshiping alongside preschoolers. The sanctuary choir includes retired adults, working adults, and an entire front row of middle-school and high-school girls. We share meals together on Wednesday nights. And most mission trips have included a wide spectrum of ages. Our children are known to members of this church by name, and the children can tell you the names of our older "living saints" in the church. What a blessing to have such a diverse mix of ages, all helping one another as we worship and serve together and grow in faith with one another.

Cullowhee Baptists are servants to one another. Not too long ago, a church member stopped by the office to say, "I was taking a meal over to so-and-so's house, and they ask that we pray for them." In many ways, the meal itself was an answer to prayer, and the person delivering the food was serving another church member in the name of Christ without having to be told to by a committee or a leader. That's called being a servant to a fellow traveler of the way. This kind of ministry among our congregation happens often. Adults each week prepare Sunday School lessons. The tea and lemonade appears ready and cold each Wednesday night. The beautiful music of our worship ministry grows from Steve Baxley's heart week after week. Meals for families after a funeral come from the gardens and homes of church members. Deacons divide the names of their church family each month and pray for us earnestly. No one is paid to do these things. We do them for one another because we care for one another.

Cullowhee Baptist cares for the community. Jackson County is home to the people we love. We live and work and worship here. As a result, we are aware of needs in the community and respond to them as best we can. Two summers ago, we had the opportunity to begin serving lunch to any child in Jackson County who was in need of food. Volunteers were eager to give a couple of hours for a summer lunch time with our community's children.

Many of us serve or have served the community through United Christian Ministries, Habitat for Humanity, Jackson Neighbors in Need, and support for the hospital chaplain. A faithful group of men, in partnership with the Council on Aging, volunteer on a regular basis to build handicap-accessible ramps at the homes of elderly residents of Jackson County. And every Super Bowl Sunday we share a soup lunch and collect money to build those ramps. Our yearly involvement in the county's Relay for Life has grown into an opportunity for fellowship as well as a ministry of hope. In addition to these hands-on ways of caring, the people of Cullowhee Baptist are known to be a people of prayer, for one another and for the community beyond us.

Cullowhee Baptist works in partnership with other Christians. Baptists have typically enjoyed what is called "voluntary associations." That is, no other Baptist church or Baptist leader (there are no Baptist bishops!) requires that we work with others in the ministry of Jesus Christ. And yet this congregation has a great many partners in ministry and mission. We have affiliated with the Cooperative Baptist Fellowship (CBF) since 1992. We are partners with the CBF of North Carolina. We joined the newly formed Western North Carolina Baptist Network (now the WNC Baptist Fellowship) in 2002 as one of the chartering congregations. We have directly supported the mission work of the Baptist World Alliance in many areas of the world. And just recently, we began to partner with Global Women to assist indigenous women in discipleship and ministry in places like Myanmar and Nepal. In other words, we work alongside Christians throughout the world in everything from cooperative worship and workshops to disaster relief missions and ministries. We know that the work of the gospel is not something we can or are willing to try to do all by ourselves. We are stronger when we work together with other churches and Christians here at home and around the world.

Cullowhee Baptist has a heart for missions. Missions and missionaries seem to be in the DNA of Baptists everywhere. It is no surprise, then, that Cullowhee Baptist takes seriously her calling to be involved in missions and the lives of missionaries wherever possible. The need for God is certainly here in Cullowhee, but that need is also found around the globe. Since 2002, this congregation has participated in mission trips to North Carolina, Arkansas, West Virginia, Alabama, Texas, Kentucky, New Jersey, South Dakota, Washington DC, Ukraine, and India. This "missions" calling is made evident through our children who just think it is the normal act of Christian love to provide animals that sustain families in developing countries through Heifer International. When church members roll bandages for a hospital in the Congo (Africa), or when Jesse Togba-Doya visits from Liberia, or when the Podgaiskys send an email update about their ministry in Ukraine, we find that it resonates with our hope of blessing the world with the gospel.

A great many individual stories are told in the pages of this book. As you read them, recognize that they are stories not so much of individual people, but of a family of faith whose purpose is to reflect the impact of God's love through Jesus Christ on this world. We offer grace and peace to all and we take the gospel out into the world as we go—this is the real treasure of Cullowhee Baptist Church.

Grace and Peace,

Tonya and Jeffrey Vickery

Some History of
Jackson County, North Carolina

From Wikipedia, the free encyclopedia

www.jacksonnc.org

Jackson County is a county located in the southwest of the U.S. state of North Carolina. As of 2010, the population was 40,271. Since 1913 its county seat has been Sylva, replacing Webster.

Major ancestry groups reported by Jackson County residents include:

· English - 14%
· Irish - 13%
· German - 13%
· American Indian tribes, specified - 10%
· Cherokee - 10%
· Scotch-Irish - 8%
· Scottish - 4%
· French (except Basque) - 2%
· Dutch - 2%
· Italian - 2%
· Black or African American - 2%
· Polish - 1%
· Welsh - 1%
· Mexican - 1%
· European - 1%
· Swedish - 1%
· Russian - 1%

HISTORY

The county was formed in 1851 from parts of Haywood County and Macon County. It was named for Andrew Jackson, President of the United States from 1829 to 1837. The original County Courts were held at the Daniel Bryson Home in the Beta Community in Scotts Creek township, and moved to Webster the following year.

In 1861 parts of Jackson County and Henderson County were combined to form Transylvania County. In 1871 parts of Jackson County and Macon County were combined to form Swain County. In 1913 Sylva became the county-seat.

Jackson County is a member of the regional Southwestern Commission council of governments. Also, Jackson County contains a portion of the Qualla Boundary, a tribal reservation for the Eastern Band of Cherokee Indians, which is subject mostly to tribal/federal laws rather than county or state laws.

The county is divided into fifteen townships:.

Barker's Creek: Named for the creek which originates and flows through the township before entering the Tuckaseigee River. It includes the Dicks Creek, Barker's Creek, and Wilmot Communities, and US 74/23 runs as a four-lane divided highway through the township.

Canada: Named for the tall ridges, narrow valleys, and sharp peaks of this part of the county, the main waterway is the East Fork of the Tuckaseigee River which flows into the River Township before joining the West Fork, becoming the Tuckaseigee River. There are four major lakes—Bear, Wolf, Tanasee Creek, and Cedar Cliff—in the township. It is served by NC 281 and is one of the most remote locations in the county.

Caney Fork: Named for the creek that flows through the township, Caney Fork, which empties into the Tuckaseigee River at East LaPorte. The main road is Caney Fork Road.

Cashiers: Named for a lost horse, the town of Cashiers is located here, as well as Panthertown Valley, Whiteside Cove, Fairfield, and Sapphire Communities. It is served by NC 107 and US 64. The Eastern Continental Divide created a ridge north of the township and defines the boundaries between the Cashiers, Canada, and Glenville townships. The Chattooga, Horsepasture, and Toxaway rivers all originate or flow through the township.

Cullowhee: The Cherokee name for the valley was corrupted from its original name into Cullowhee. The original either means "Valley of the Lilies" or "Valley of the Buzzards." The "Valley of the Lilies" nickname is more commonly referred to. NC 107, Old NC 107, and NC 107-Alternate all serve the township as major roads, though NC 107 is the only four-lane roadway. Western Carolina University, Speedwell Community, The Village of Forest Hills, Old Cullowhee Road Community, Buzzards Roost Community, and Dicks Gap Community are all within the township. It is one of the first areas to be settled by the whites, along with Caney Fork, River, Scotts Creek, and Canada townships. It is the largest township population-wise according to the 2000 United States Census. The Tuckaseigee River and Cullowhee Creek both flow through the township, with the latter emptying into the former around Old Cullowhee Road *(see page vii for more information on Cullowhee).*

Dillsboro: Named after the Dills Family who founded the town, the township is home to the town of Dillsboro. To the northwest of Dillsboro, Scotts Creek, which flows from the Scotts Creek Township through the Sylva Township into Dillsboro township, empties into the Tuckaseigee River. US 74/23, US 441, and NC 107 all converge in two major intersections within the township.

Greens Creek: Named for the creek which flows through most of the township before emptying into Savannah Creek, Greens Creek township is served by US 441, in the form of a four-lane highway along the western edge. Greens

Creek Road goes through the middle of the township.

Hamburg: Named for the fort and original name of Glenville, the township is served by NC 107. The area was once a large valley, but the valley was flooded in 1941 to form Lake Glenville. The West Fork of the Tuckaseigee River originates within the township and flows north into the River township.

Mountain: Named for Cullowhee Mountain which it resides on, the Mountain Township is served by NC 107-Alternate. The headwaters of Cullowhee Creek are located here; the creek flows north into Cullowhee Township before joining the Tuckaseigee River.

Qualla: Named for the Qualla Boundary, which takes up a lion's share portion of the township, the Qualla Township is served by US 441, US 19, and US 74/23. Smokey Mountain Elementary School, located in the township,resulted from the 1980 consolidation of Qualla Elementary School and Log Cabin Association Consolidated School. The communities of Qualla, Birdtown, Soco, Whittier, Indian Hills, and Wilmot are all located at least partially, if not wholly, within the township.

River: Named for the Tuckaseigee River, which converges from two streams into one within the township, is served by NC 107 and NC 281. The Tuckasegee Community is located in the township.

Savannah: Named for Savannah Creek, which runs through the district, Savannah Township is home to the Viewpoint, Pumpkintown, Savannah, and Fort Wilderness communities. The township is served by four-lane US 441.

Scotts Creek: Named for Scotts Creek, which begins and flows through the township before running into the Sylva township. It is served by US 74/23 and old US 19/23, which run through the five communities within the township: Balsam, Willets, Ochre Hill, Addie, and Beta. The Murphy Branch Railroad also runs through the township.

Sylva: Named for William D. Sylva, the town of Sylva is also named for him. The township is home to the town of Sylva and is served by NC 107, US 74/23, and BUS 23. The Jackson County Courthouse and Library are both located in the township. Scotts Creek runs through the township before emptying into Dillsboro Township.

Webster: The location of the town of Webster, Webster Township sits at the original geographical center of the county, which has in fact moved to Cullowhee Township due to land taken away for the formation of Swain and Transylvania counties. It was for many years home to the only town in Jackson County. It is served by NC 116 and NC 107. The county-seat designation and courthouse were located here from 1851–1913, but Sylva stole the county-seat designation away from Webster.

Reflection

From all of these communities have come members of Cullowhee Baptist

Church. The people who settled Jackson County came before it was even a county and brought with them the desire to worship God. They persevered from place to place, always following the river, until they found a home in Cullowhee Valley. Then, as time went on, members from Cullowhee Baptist Church spread out through Jackson County, establishing many other community Baptist churches *(see page 36)*.

More about the Settlement of Cullowhee

Nestled along a mountain river and in a wide valley along a creek, Cullowhee is one of the oldest settlements in Jackson County and reportedly had the first school in the area, a one-room school in 1830. The area was largely farmland, which was cleared in the 1800s. Today many farms are wooded or have homes or university buildings built on them. William H. (or Major Billy) Bryson opened the first post office in Cullowhee. The name of the post office was East La Porte (French for Eastern Portage or Gate), and it was built under a chestnut tree in the bend of the river. A bold spring gushed out of the mountain there, and it was a stopping place for travelers of the little dirt road that followed closely by the river banks. After the establishment of Cullowhee school, it became necessary to consolidate the exsisting post offices, so in 1883, Painter Post Office was founded by Rolling A. Painter, and became the consolidated post office, located in his store. This led to the further development of the Old Cullowhee Road area into a business district. The post office was renamed Cullowhee in 1908, taking over from another post office in the vicinity of Forest Hills. In 1889, Cullowhee High School, today's Western Carolina University, was founded by Robert Lee Madison. The institution ceased to be named a high school when the first brick graded school opened in 1923 with grades 1-11. It was locted on the site of the former Brown Cafeteria Building.

In 1940, a massive flood caused severe damage to the business district, wiping away almost all the buildings on the side of the river opposite Western Carolina University, the north side of the river. The buildings on the opposite side of the river survived, though waterlogged. The flood crested at 21 feet (6.4 m) above Cullowhee Dam, the highest on record. Today such a flood would be impossible because of the dams built on the East and West forks of the Tuckaseigee River. When the area rebuilt, the buildings clung to the higher

The Old Cullowhee Road area of Cullowhee in the 1920s. Along the Tuckaseigee River this area became home to the Painter Store and Post Office in 1883, and commercial/ residential development sprung up in the area. The Post Office became known as Cullowhee in 1908, and the old Cullowhee Post Office near Forest Hills was discontinued. The Painter Store and a neighboring store did well enough that in the 1920s they built new buildings. The old Painter Store was the site of the Village Store. (Photo: Richard Kenni, 1920)

The old Cullowhee School, built in 1923 and shown here about that time. This building was a school for 16 years until 1939 and later made way for Brown Cafeteria on the Western Carolina University Campus in 1955. (Photo: Richard Kenni, 1923)

ground around Old Cullowhee Road and the area closer to the river was abandoned. Many of these newer buildings are today in poor shape. The area underwent massive growth starting in the 1960s and continuing through today; it will continue into the future with plans for a new University Town Center, Old Cullowhee Road revitalization, and many new homes being built or planned for the area.

Since 1923, the town has had a public school, which has moved through four different buildings over the years. Cullowhee Valley School is the latest incarnation of this school. Before Cullowhee Valley, the public school was Cordelia Camp Laboratory School from 1964 until 1994, McKee Training School from 1939 until 1964, and Cullowhee Training School from 1923 until 1939. The two former buildings still stand on the university campus, but the latter was demolished in the 1950s.

Most towns the size of Cullowhee have a downtown, shopping area/ district, and grocery store, but Cullowhee really doesn't have any of that, because what it did have as a downtown area was washed away by the flood of 1940.

Some History
Leading up to the Establishment of Cullowhee Baptist Church

Elder Humphrey Posey (1780–1846)
Excerpt taken from *Sketch of the life of Elder Humphrey Posey*
by Robert Fleming, 1797–1880
University Library, University of North Carolina at Chapel Hill

From the days of John the Baptist until now, the Baptists have been more famous for preaching in the wilderness, than for wearing soft rainment, and for dwelling in king's houses. They have generally been looked upon as reeds shaken with the wind, and have everywhere been spoken against. Many of them have been eloquent ministers of Jesus Christ, "fervent in the spirit, and mighty in the scriptures," and have "taught diligently the things of the Lord." Some of the most distinguished men which the world has ever known were in principle and profession Baptists.

This is true of Elder Humphrey Posey, Here are his words:

"I obtained license to preach in Union District, South Carolina, in 1803, and in 1804 removed to Buncombe County, North Carolina, on account of bad health. On the third day of August, I preached my first sermon there. I then went preaching about through 'the hill country,' inviting sinners to come to the Saviour;—telling them the way of salvation through the Redeemer.

"In 1805, I commenced preaching, in evenings, in a destitute settlement, near where I was teaching a school on Cane Creek. Brother James Whitaker and myself drew up Articles of Faith, as we could not find any in the country; and we collected all the members intending to be in the constitution, and examined them on the Articles. All being agreed, a presbytery was invited to attend. The presbytery was pleased with our Articles of Faith, and so the church was organized."

Coming from the same area as Elder humphrey Posey, Adam Corn, for whom Posey served as mentor, began his ministry about 1818. He helped to establish what eventually became Cullowhee Baptist Church.

Elder Adam Corn (1783–1871)

Adam Corn was born May 2, 1783 and was one of THE first Baptist ministers in the area. He came from the family of John Peter and Elizabeth Parr Corn. Adam was the grandson of Mathew and Molly Corn of Albemarle Co, Virginia and of John and Miriam Parr of Henry Co, Va.

Hannah Heatherly, Adam's wife, was born in Pendleton District, S.C., about 1791; the daughter of John Heatherly and granddaughter of George Heatherly.

Adam was ordained in 1812 at Mud Creek Baptist Church, Henderson Co. NC. The church was organized by Adam's brother, Noah Parr Corn, in 1804.

Adam and Hannah Corn were solid citizens of their community, devout and highly respected. Here are SOME of their children: John, born 1813, Alfred born 1817, Silas born 1824, Jesse born 1825, Adam Posey born 1833, Jacob, Newton, Mary Ann.

Hannah Corn died February 8, 1859; Adam followed September 12, 1871. They are buried in Lower Bell Creek Cemetery near Hiawasse, Ga. *(See page 18 for more information.)*

Locust Old Field Baptist Church
"Mother Church" to Cullowhee Baptist Church

In 1803, a dedicated missionary named "Elder" Humphrey Posey provided the organizational skills to bring the belivers together to form a church in the community called Fort Pigeon. This spiritual community was known as Locust Old Field Baptist, after the hilltop site on which the present day Locust Old Field Cemetery is located.

Locust Old Field Baptist Church is the first of any denomination established west of Asheville. This building of rough-hewn logs was demolished just before the Civil War and was replaced with a framed and weather boarded structure.

Early believers at Locust Old Field had a commitment to the great commission and to Western North Carolina. The thirteen charter members had grown to seventy-eight by the year 1812. This number included slaves who had been baptized into the fellowship.

The Locust Old Field Baptist Church has been termed the "Mother Church" of all Baptist Churches served by the Haywood Association.

Actural first page of Cullowhee Baptist Church Minutes

Written November 17, 1821

(Transcribed)

November 17, 1821

Members of Locust Old Field Church
Dismissed in order to become a Constitution
met at Tuckesegee Meeting House, Viz.

James Stiles	Jane Stiles
Benjamin Hatfield	Martha Buchanan
Thomas Stiles	Jaley Hibbards
James Buchanan	Sarah Mason
Henry Wood	Nancy Buchanan

Other members dismissed from Locust
Old Field failing to attend after
Preaching by Brother Corn
Enquired for the fellowship of the members
presant and found a union breatheren Adam
Corn & Joseph Byers from Crabtree Church
presented them selvs as a presbytery to
examine in to their strenth to become a
constitution
we the members before named without
any writen principles presented to the
presbytery unitedly take the scriptures as our
rule of faith and practice after satisfaction
obtained by the presbytery respectin the
soundness of
our faith and was considered with sufficient
strength to become a constitution presented
breatheren James Stiles & benjamin E. Hatfield
as our choice to act as deacons who wer
examined
and ordaind & wer by the presbytery
pronounced
a church of Jesus Christ of the baptist faith in
order by the name of Unity.
first appointed B. E. Hatfield Clerk 2nd
opened a door for the reseption of members

______

Sabeth rcd. Edward Dailey John Gibel
Mary Stiles Susanah Hatfield Hannah Strain
Margaret Buchanan and ___ ____ all by letter

Some History of
Cullowhee Baptist Church Throughout the Years

by John Bell

Excerpts by Barbara Dooley—Samples of some of the earliest recordings of the church

(Note: Some names are left out and replaced with [a man] and [a woman])

In 1821 the Cherokee lands west of the Balsams had just opened for settlement. On November 17 some ten members of the Locust Old Field Church near Waynesville were dismissed to "become a Constitution" at the "Tuckasegee Meeting House." These charter members of the new "Unity Baptist Church" were James, Jane, and Thomas Stiles; Martha, James, and Nancy Buchanan; Benjamin Hatfield; Jaley Hibbards; Sarah Mason; and Henry Wood.

The minutes described the process for creating this new church (quoting): "Enquired for the fellowship of members present and found a union breatheren Adam Com & Joseph Byers from Crabtree Church presented themselves as a presbytery to examine in to their strength to become a constitution we the members before named. without any written principles. presented to the presbytery unitedly take the scriptures as our rule of faith and practice after satisfaction obtained by the presbytery respectin the soundness of our faith and was considered with sufficient strength to become a constitution. presented breathern James Stiles and Benjamin E. Hatfield as our choice to act as deacons who wer examined and ordained & wer by the presbytery pemounced a church of Jesus Christ of the Baptist faith and order by the name of Unity:-"

Excerpt from the original minutes:

1821, p. 2:

15 Dec 1821 New members: Peter and Mary Mason

1822

16 Feb 1822 New members: Edward Chastain

16 Mar 1822 New member: Benjamin Stiles

20 Apr 1822 New members: Lucy Stiles; Arty Bryson

18 May 1822 New member: Hannah Chastain

15 Jun 1822 New member: Joseph Buchanan; Margaret Quary 20 Jul 1822 New members: Adam Corn, Hannah Corn; Margaret Hooper

---

The new church met in the Tuckaseigee Meeting House, a log building near the mouth of Love Branch near Webster. The first minister was Adam Com of Henderson County, just ordained in 1818. The church requested Adam Corn to take the pastoral care of the church, and he accepted (he pastored until 1840). They appointed Brother Chastain "to site [sic] Peter Mason and his wife with Sarah Mason to attend next meeting to give the church satisfaction for their neglect of attending church meetings."

Excerpt from the original minutes:

1822

16 Nov 1822 [a man] is found in disorder and is laid under censure until next meeting.

14 Dec 1822 [a man] is releast from the charge against him. Peter Mason came forward and gave satisfaction for the charge against him and the women.

1823, p. 3

March, 1823 New member: Naoma Brown

October, 1823 [a man] charged with excessive drinking and unbecoming language. Will be cited to be at next meeting.

1824, p. 4

18 Jan 1824 [a man] came forward and gave satisfaction of the charge against him.

20 Mar 1824 Church ordered the clerk to wright [sic] brother [a man] to sit with us at next meeting.

17 Apr 1824 Brother [a man] came forward and gave satisfaction for his long absence.

17 Apr 1824 New member: Robert Shipp

18 Apr 1824 New members: Joseph and Mary Simons

15 May 1824 Church agreed to celebrate the Lord's Supper the next day.

16 May 1824 New members: Elizabeth and Cintha Shipp

1 Jul 1824 Adam Corn, James Stiles, and Benjamin E. Hatfield chosen as delegates to the Association.

August, 1824 [a man] charges himself with intoxication—case laid over. Joseph Simons and James Stiles appointed to invite Brothe [a man] to attend next meeting and give satisfaction for his long absence.

1824, p. 5

August, 1824 New member: Clark Coody

In 1824 the church adopted the articles of faith and rules of decorum of the French Broad Association of which it was a member.

December meeting "disappointed." (This is the word used when no meeting is held.)

Blacks were early members of the church. Coming as converts in 1824 were "black Bob," "black Jude," and "black Sookey." The latter was the handmaid of James B. Love. In 1827 "black Dinnah" joined as a convert. After the Civil War black members left to join a church of their own in Webster. Malinda Love, the last black member, departed in 1875. In the 1960s the church tried again to welcome blacks as the college student body became integrated.

Excerpt from the original minutes:

1824, p. 5

Aug meeting, 1824 "next received by Exspeariance, Black Bob"

1826, p. 8

Mar 18, 1826 Church appointed Robert Shipp and William Poteet "to cite black brother Bob to attend next meeting"

Apr 15, 1826 "The case of Black Brother Bob taken up and satisfaction obtained.

1827, p. 10

Jun 4, 1827 Church received "Black Diannah by Exspeariance"

Aug 5, 1827 p. 11 Received "Black Jude by Exspeariance"

1828, p. 16

Mar 22, 1828 Received "Black Sookey, John B. Love's handmaid by Exspeariance."

By 1826 most church members must have lived in Cullowhee Valley. In that year the brethren at the "Mouth of Colowhee" were empowered to transact business for the church. Then on December 18, 1830, the members agreed to "Remove the government of this Church to Cullowhee Meeting House and Call the Name of this Church Cullowhee." This meeting house was a log building near the mouth of Cullowhee Creek. It was frequently flooded.

The church grew slowly. It had only twenty members in 1862. Families represented were the Brysons, Joneses, Watsons, Wilsons, Sheltons, Morrisons, Longs, Russells, Hyatts, and Pressleys. The membership numbered 100 in 1885 and 381 in 1955.

One of the reasons for slow growth was the creation of new churches. Members came from a wide area, and travel was difficult. The early members lived the length of the Tuckaseigee and Oconoluftee river valleys. In 1828 some thirty-four members left to form the "Ochonia Luftia" church. A building of this church still stands near Smokemont. In 1830, Daniel Bryson and others left to start the Scotts Creek Baptist Church. In 1836 the Parkers, Hoopers, Catheys. Websters, and Cowards withdrew to form a new church, presumably at Caney Fork. Caney Fork Baptist Church evolved into the Tuckaseigee Baptish Church. Other churches founded from Cullowhee included: Old Savannah Baptist (circa 1836); Speedwell Baptist (circa 1902), Little Savannah Baptist (circa 1914), and Black Mountain Baptist Church. *(See page 36 for more information.)*

The early church existed on the frontier. Much lawlessness prevailed. The church tried to maintain proper standards of social conduct. It occasionally dismissed members for improper behavior. This included false swearing, profanity, dancing, card playing, making whiskey, bastardy, chronic absenteeism, stealing, drunkenness, and adultery. (By 1925 this function had passed to the Board of Deacons, which heard cases in secret. Today, the church no longer sanctions disciplining members even by the Board of Deacons.)

Excerpt from the original minutes:

1839, p. 33

10 Jun 1839 Meeting held at Richard Wilson's
New member: William Wilson
13 Jul 1839 The church met in order and fellowship was not found. [a man] reported himself to be guilty of taken some potatoes contrary to what the church thinks good order. Laid the case over until next meeting. Appointed sisters Sintha Wood & Sarah Wilson to site [sic] his wife to attend as Evidence. A Corn, B.Kerby, Michael Long, Wm. Carson, and E. Underwood delegates to Association. Wm. Carson to write the church letter.
10 Aug 1839 Fellowship not found. [a man] and his wife were excluded for disobedience in failing to attend. Dissatisfaction was found between [a man] and [a man]. Laid under censure till next meeting.
4 Sep 1839 The censured Brethren talked together and the matter was adjusted to satisfaction. They were

restored to fellowship and [a man] to his clerk's office.

1841, P. 39

9 Oct 1841 Sister [a woman] came forward and gave satisfaction for her absence. Bro. [a man] proclaimed a disfellowship against old Bro. [a man] and [a woman] for hard talk and circulating tales to his prejudice.

True to Baptist principles, the Unity Baptist Church joined associations of other churches. The purpose was to assist one another in matters of faith and practice. In 1822 the church joined the French Broad Association. Then in 1829 Humphrey Posey, one of the great frontier Baptist preachers, helped form the Tuckaseigee Baptist Association. Unity Baptist joined it, and Cullowhee Baptist became a member.

The eartiest church officers were deacons. The first two were James Stiles and Benjamin Hatfield (1821). Other early deacons and the dates of their selection were William Cathey (1830), William Parker (1832), James B. and Michael Long (1837), G. Falls and W. Carson (1837), and William Watson and Daniel Bryson (1853). Until the 1920s deacons were selected for life. Thereafter they were elected for fixed terms and rotated out of office at regular times. At first only men served as deacons, but on 26 Jun 1966 Lucy Crawford was elected as the first woman deacon, with Maxie Freeman elected soon thereafter.

Deacons assisted the minister with church business and with communion and baptism. In 1822 the church had communion once a year; in 1840 twice a year. In 1927 the church voted to have communion monthly, then for decades it

Lucy Crawford
1st woman deacon

was quarterly, then came back to monthly in 2000. In early years footwashing accompanied communion. It was a ceremony that symbolized the role of humble servant. The first record of footwashing was in 1823 and the last in 1841.

Maxie Freeman

Other church officers were clerk and treasurer. The first clerk was Benjamin Hatfield, appointed in 1821. In 1840 the church "appointed" Enoch Underwood as clerk and also treasurer. Starting in 1922 the church for the first time elected an annual slate of officers. These were E. H. Stillwell, clerk; R. L. Duckett, treasurer; Nancy Brown, local treasurer for the Southern Baptist Convention, treasurer for the $75 million fund; Mr. Mull, janitor; and R. L. Duckett, Sunday School superintendent.

The minister was the central officer in the church, helping the people's spiritual growth. In the early days the minister worked at a regular job like farming and preached part-time. The church elected him annually. One minister sometimes had four churches at the same time. He preached once a month at each church. For most of the 1800s the Cullowhee church met only monthly. The earliest ministers were not well educated. In 1866 the Tuckaseigee Association urged that churches not license men to preach until they had the "rudiments of an English education.... " The Association recommended a course of study in religion and theology, but no college degree was required. Starting in the 1920s, practically all ministers had some formal college and theological education.

The church minutes do not always accurately indicate who the minister was. *(A list of the ministers can be found on page 19)*. To accommodate a minister the church built the first parsonage in 1922. This indicated that the church expected the ministry to be full-time. This parsonage was a wood frame building that faced the dam on the river.

In 1965 the church tore down the old parsonage and built a brick house on the same site.

Excerpt from the original minutes:

29 Aug 1965

THE NEW PARSONAGE

"The building and dedication of the parsonage is an occasion for thanksgiving and rejoicing, for it enables the church to extend its Christian ministry throughout the region.

The new parsonage was contracted for $20,280.00, but this amount does not reflect the value of additional improvements. The face of the parsonage lot was lifted in order to obtain as much flat land as possible; cost $657.19. Storm windows were installed for $228.00. The brick walls and steps and concrete walkways cost an additional $750.00. Creek-bed gravel was laid on the drive and parking area for $238.00. Grass planting and proper

Church Congregation in old church (circa 1920s) — *Photo supplied by Ruth Bryson*
Her mother, Evie Phillips Ensley is on the far right, top row, holding a child

drainage of the yard cost an additional $100. A concrete landing, driveway drainage, parking area wall, and asphalt drive cost approximately $1,400.00. The total cost of the parsonage with all these improvements is about $24,000.00.

We can be thankful that we have been given the means to pay cash for all of the additional improvements and $7,365.90 toward the $20,280.00 cost of the parsonage."

The establishment of the Cullowhee School in 1888 and its direction by Robert Lee Madison in 1889 opened a new ministry for the church. The early relationship between the new educational community and the church is sketchy. In 1890 the church permitted Madison to use the church for music and art classes until he completed a building. In 1895 Madison reimbursed the church for windows his students broke playing ball. In 1927 the church sold a sixth of an acre to the school for $100. In 1929 the school gave the church a half acre of land on which to erect a new building. Over the years a cooperative relationship continued.

The nearness of the school made the church aware of the need to minister to students. *(More on ministering to college students on page 47.)* The small church lacked the resources to do all that was needed. Starting in 1916 the church began applying for aid from the Mission Board from the state Baptist Convention. At first it asked for only $250. The money enabled the church to secure a full-time minister, probably W. F. West, and start a full-time church program. The need to accommodate more students led to church building programs in 1919 and 1929. The Southern Baptist Home Mission Board gave the church $500 toward the 1919 building. The need to serve even more students led Western Carolina Teachers College President Hiram T. Hunter to head a $30,000 church building program in 1929. Despite aid from the state convention, the depression made it impossible to complete the building until the 1940s. The convention gave about a third of the cost and continued to give money to help pay the minister. In 1962 the church no longer needed help from the convention, and it stood on its own financially.

Excerpt from the original minutes:

1892

16 Sep 1892, p. 43, A collection of $10.60 was taken up for the minister.
p. 47, Collection of $2.00 taken up for A. B. Thomas, who preached that day.

1893

21 Oct 1893 Agreed to pay Bro. Thomas $131.00 as salary for ?th his time.

1894

21 April 1894,p. 50 Made a contract with W. H. rich to preach Saturday and Sunday once a month and to visit some. Salary would be $75 a year to be paid monthly.

The church also worked closely with the state convention's Baptist Student Union, an organization to help Baptist students in college settings. The first mention of this program is in the 1942 minutes. Then the church offered the BSU use of a "prayer shack" on church property. The first full-time BSU director came about 1960. He was Colin Godwin, and he used the church building for his programs. The church supported the move to construct a BSU building on church property. This was done in 1965. Other BSU directors were Joseph Clontz, Joe David Fore, Winston Hardman, and Wanda Kidd, first woman director (*see page 60*).

The Sunday School was another important church ministry to students. Although the Tuckaseigee Association encouraged the founding of Sunday Schools in the 1830s and 1840s, the church did nothing until later. In 1881 the church appointed Robert L. Watson a delegate to a "Sabbath School Convention." Then in 1893 the Rev. A. H. Sims held a convention in Cullowhee. Thereafter the church offered a Sunday School. In the 1890s the church offered Sunday Schools in outlying areas like Weyehutta and Speedwell. Not until 1920 was the Sunday School officially organized with a superintendent heading it. In 1930 the Sunday School was a thriving concern with eighteen classes, about a third for college-age students.

The church established other programs to help train members. The Baptist Young People's Union got started in 1922. In the 1940s it evolved into the Baptist Training Union for all ages. The Daily Vacation Bible School started in 1928.

Excerpt from the original minutes:

1928

April 1, 1928 p. 110 "Without motion, Bro. Stafford was authorized to go ahead with plans for Daily Vacation Bible School."

1929

Jan 6, 1929, p. 114 Church voted to support Vacation Bible School again in 1929.

1936

Sept 13, 1936 Bible school held Sept 7-11. 59 enrolled. "Boys were taught Bible Lessons and manual training. Girls were given lessons from the Bible and lessons in domestic science."

The continued existence of this body of Christian believers indicates an inner necessity to worship God. But they changed times and forms of worship to meet practical needs. The 1800s saw the church meeting monthly on a Saturday for business and on Sunday for worship. Not until the early 1900s did Cullowhee have weekly Sunday worship. The forms of worship changed also. At first foot washing, a ceremony symbolizing the humble servant, and communion were held in conjunction, but before the Civil War, foot washing ceased. Communion has always been held at regular intervals, sometimes semi-annually, sometimes monthly, sometimes quarterly. Converts have always been immersed in water. Until 1929 all baptisms were held in creeks and rivers, winter and summer, but a baptistery in the present building permits indoor baptism. In the 1800s converts related emotional experiences connected with their conversion, but this practice has died out.

Another form of worship was the revival, its major purpose being the winning of converts. While revivals are mentioned in the 1870s, they did not become a standard annual feature until the 1890s. In recent years the revival has declined in usage for evangelism. Personal evangelism and the Christain responsibility for helping alleviate the great social problems of our time are now included in the broad scope of evangelism.

Excerpt from the original minutes:

1892

16 Sep 1892, p. 42. New members: Phillip Henson, Tillie Potts, and Mary Mills. The meeting was "at Watter Edg," and they were baptized that day.

1894

25 Aug 1894, p. 52. New members: Bro. Basel, Mackey Brown, and Jessee Brown; Sister Tishey Bishop. A woman said she had done wrong and ask the church to forgive her. They did and received her to Fellowship. On Sunday they met "at the Watter," and the new members were baptized. Then met at the House for preaching.

The first mention of a music program appears in the 1890 minutes when S. W. Henson was appointed a "Singing Cleark." In the 1940s and 1950s H.P. Smith and Jack Barnette developed an extensive choir program. Ed vom Lehn became the first trained music director in 1958. *(More on the music history on page 40.)*

Selected excerpts from the original minutes:

1890

April 5, 1890, p. 31 S.W. Henson apptd. "Singing Cleark for twelve months."

1897

Aug 21, 1897, p. 67 "Opened services by reading a pertion of God's word and singing and prayer."

1912

July 21, 1912, p. 44 Dismissed the service by singing the Doxology.

1929

January 6, 1929, 110 hymnals purchased for $74.68. Title: "The Modern Hymnal."

1939

December 17, 1939. deacons meeting: "A motion was made to approach M.A. Huggins as to the possibility of securing a young man to direct music in church and serve as pastor's assistant in other ways, with the idea of jointly paying his expenses in college as compensation for his work to the amount of $150.00. The motion carried."

Relations with the Methodist church have been good over the years. Before 1880 a church member could be dismissed for attending another church. That attitude changed. In 1890 the church let the Methodists meet in the church building instead of the schoolhouse for their quarterly meetings. In 1905 the Methodist minister, U. L. Marsh, helped with the church's revival. In 1918-1919 the Cullowhee Baptist Church met in the Methodist building while its own building was under construction. Then in 1936 Cullowhee Baptists let the Methodists use their building while the Methodist church building was under construction. They even gave the Methodists $121 toward their building.

Perhaps the most frequent word is the minutes is "fellowship." Apparently, everyone present was asked at the beginning of the meeting if the members were in fellowship, ie, "...was there good will among them."

Excerpt from the original minutes:

1870

21 May, 1870, p. 72. Cullowhee Baptist Church met and on inquiry found the members present in fellowship."

1925

August 9, 1925. p. 89. Com. apptd. to prepare a program for decoration day.

1933

November 5, 1933, p. 198. Church decided to have regular every-member canvass. It was decided also to have an "annual church and family reunion day when all the members come out and bring dinner and spend the day in fellowshipping and renewing acquaintance." Pledge cards wd. be issued to persons attending.

Missions has been an integral part of Cullowhee Baptist Church from it's inception. Dating back as far as 1889, the minutes show the funding of "Missions." *(More on Missions" on page 48.)*

Excerpt from the original minutes:

1890

4 Jan 1890, p. 29.p. 36. An offering of $3.17 taken up for foreign missions.

5 Oct 1890 A collection of $2.25 was taken up for conventional missions.

1892

25 Jun 1892, p. 41. A collection of $2.32 was taken up for conventional missions.

22 Jul 1892 A collection of 92 cents was taken up for the orphanage.

To support its expanding programs, the church had to provide regular financial support. It adopted its first budget in 1919, a total of $144, of which $117 was the minister's salary. The budget grew to $2,520 in 1924.

In February, 1927, I.K. Stafford was elected pastor. Then, one year later, with help from the Baptist General Board in Raleigh, the church began the process of building a new church. On April 29, 1929, the church received the deed for the plot of ground adjacent to its present site. The State of North Carolina had conveyed a lot for the new Baptist Church from lands belonging to Cullowhee State Normal School. Then in May of 1929, Pastor Stafford was authorized to appoint a committee to provide for the laying of the cornerstone for the new church. On motion it was ordered that "Cullowhee Baptist Church" be inscribed on the part of the stone facing the road and that "Organized 1821, Erected in 1929" be inscribed on the end of the stone on the side facing the old church. Mr. Stein of Sylva gifted his work on the marble cornerstone. He charged nothing except the price of the marble.

The old church material was first offered to Wolf Creek Church, who advised that they were not financially in shape to build and hence would not be interested, but appreciated very much the offer. On October 4, 1931, the old church sold to Eric Coward for $210. Pastor Stafford paid $150 to Jackson County Bank and $60 to Sylva Coal and Lumber Company.

Selected excerpts from the original minutes:

1928

November 4, 1928. Matter of janitor discussed. Hired Garland Franks to build fires at a salary of $5.00 a month.

1929

August 4 1929. On motion it was orderd that "Cullowhee Baptist Church" be inscribed on the part of the stone facing the road and that "Organized 1821, Erected in 1929" be inscribed on the end of stone on side facing old church. Mr. Stein of Sylva will donate his work, charging only for the cost of the marble.

1929

November 10, 1929. It was decided to try to raise $1000 and borrow another thousand from the bank and go forward with the work on the new church.

1930

October 5, 1930. Long list of new members including Johnny Clayton and Cordelia Camp. Pastor Stafford reported he had gathered cull lumber and scraps enough to build a chicken house. The church did not feel inclined to make any charge for this material.

1944 Side View of Cullowhee Baptist Church

On August 15-17, 1929, The Tuckaseigee Baptist Association met with Cullowhee Baptist Church to celebrate the One Hundredth Anniversary of the Association and the Cornerstone Laying for the New Church building at Cullowhee. On August 17, 1929, at 10am, after a devotional by Rev. John Hoglen, the Corner Stone laying was accompanied by the song, "How Firm A Foundation." Placing of the stone was by T.C. Ledbetter and R.L. Bryson, members of the Building Committee, assisted by W. R. Painter, mason. Prayer was by Rev. T. F. Deitz. Addresses in the afternoon were "Looking Backward," Rev. A. V. Joyner, and "Looking Forward," by Rev. W. F. West.

The church budget rose to $5,100 in 1931, declined to $1,115 in 1935, then jumped to $10,850 in 1960, and over $100,000 in 1990.

In 1989, the Rev. Joseph Yelton, a Westem Carolina University graduate and at the time pastor for three years of Cullowhee Baptist Church, produced a concise overview of the year 1989. Following are excerpts from his report:

"State of Cullowhee Baptist Church—1989"

Dollars and Cents: You folk met your 1988 budget of $88,000.00 by the skin of your teeth. You then raised the budget to $103,000.00 in 1989. As I write this article (December 11), you have given almost $94,000 toward the unified budget. Will we be able to come up with the remaining $9,000 in the final three Sundays of the year? I rejoice in your faithfulness, for with utter assurance I can tell you will give better than $10,000 more to the unified budget this year than last. That doesn't include the thousands you have given to C.T.B., Lottie Moon, special offerings, etc. You will probably finish out the unified budget year at $100,000 plus.

Honduras: From February 18 - March 4 of 1989, our church sponsored the third year running a construction mission team to the city of San Pedro Sula. Our eleven-member team was told at the end their progress in two weeks time has never been equaled in 15 years of volunteer efforts. (As a footnote, the church meeting in that building baptized over 40 people since April of '89.)

Fellowship: This past year we have had more hiking and camping trips than lots of outdoors clubs. We have shared fellowships with other churches. We have eaten meals, sat by the lake, jumped on the trampoline, and partied with the best of them. Our volleyball team nearly had a perfect season...we ruined that by winning one.

Wednesday Evening Meal and Bible Study: Perhaps the greatest gain in enthusiasm and actual countable warm bodies has been this phase of our ministry. We averaged around 70 to 80 for the meal, with about two-thirds of that number remaining for the Bible Study and Children's Ministry. Praise God!

Community Care Ministry: This past year a Vacation Bible School was offered the Community Care folk for the first-time ever. Several of the residents made first time professions of faith, including Mr. L.C. Wilson who just recently went home to be with the Lord. Lora Ponder has taken this Community Care Ministry under her able care and thereby, God has blessed. The Sunday School attendance has tripled, and the van now runs regularly to have as many as will, attend all our church activities.

Jackson County Jail Ministry: This past year 14 men and one woman gave their lives over to the Lordship of Jesus by way of this ministry. Weekly, some of our laity leaders go to the jail on Wednesdays for mid-week visitation and then on Sundays for Bible teaching. For the first time, we have rejoiced that some of the ex-inmates are sharing the regular life of our church. "For I was imprisoned and you visited me."

Vacation Bible School: Our church sponsored three Vacation Bible Schools this year—a morning, evening and mission VBS. This accounts for our all time record enrollment of 165 with a total average attendance of 119. Ten made professions of faith. We are endebted to Irene Hooper and a host of good support people for the ministry given.

Rotation Visitation: These ministers have made over 200 in home, face to face visits this past year. The ministry wrought here is incalculable.

College Student Ministry: We gladly accept our posture as a mission church...a church on mission to the WCU campus (approximately 7,000 strong). Steve Baxley and the College Committee have done what we thought impossible with 1989's participation exceeding the strides of '88. Our treasurer, Annie Hoyle, tells me that significant dollar amounts are coming into the church by way of these students, a first in her time as treasurer. But best of all, check the ministry these gifted students extended to us by their involvement in the ministry to the jail, the Sunday School, our youth and children, the music ministry, etc., etc., etc.. Praise God from Whom all blessings flow.

And to add to all of this: The *Week of the Family* given in 1989, the *Suicide Seminar*, the involvement of 20 in *Masterlife Training*, the 16 kids blessed in *The Christmas Store*, the many blessed by our laity involvement in *United Christian Ministries of Jackson Couty*, the 24 families fed by our *XYZ Club* at Thanksgiving, the 14 families given groceries in *White Christmas*, the *Samaritan's Purse* project led in our church by Polly Rice where we collected hundreds of shoe boxes for *Operation Christmas Child*, and on and on and on!

History Sketch of the Tuckaseigee Baptist Association (1829)

Organized November 6, 1829, at Cullowhee Meeting House by delegates from Locust Old Field, Waynesville, Cullowhee, Mount Zion, Cowee, and Head of Tennessee churches, the Tuckaseigee Baptist Association included territrory extending from Madison County to Rabun County, Georgia. In 1859 the association formed the Tuckaseigee United Baptist Book Society to supply the local need for Bibles. Four years later it established Tuckaseigee Baptist High School, Holly Springs, to train ministers. Churches withdrew to form county associations, Haywood (1886) and Macon (1903), until in 1954, only Jackson County churches remained.

The Last Ten Years

In the past decade the church has made many improvements to the building. About 2002 the heating system was updated, and old windows were replaced with new thermal windows. A new parking area was graded and paved at the rear of the building. The continued use of the kitchen for Wednesday night meals and other social functions made improvements in the kitchen imperative. In 2007, using the plans drawn by a committee made up of those women using the kitchen the most, architect Odell Thompson drew plans to code and presented plans for remodeling the kitchen and fellowship hall. These plans were approved, and the work was completed in 2007. As part of this project, the old bathrooms were improved and a new one constructed. Also, the fellowship hall was completely remodeled with new ceiling, lighting, cabinets, furniture, and tile floor. To make the building safer, fire doors were installed in the stairways. This construction cost about $250,000 and necessitated borrowing $100,000, but the note was soon paid off. In 1988 ceiling fans were installed in the auditorium, but by 2011 they proved inadequate for the warmer summers. After many informal conversations about the possibility of air conditioning the sanctuary, the King's Daughters Bible Class officially established the Air Conditioning Fund with their contribution of $1,000 in August of 2008. Some smaller gifts had been made previously, but this action by the King's Daughters made the statement that many members of the congregation were serious about going forward. Contributions continued to come in randomly until a pledge drive in late 2010 encouraged congregation members to make a three-year commitment (or a one-time donation) to raise funds for the project. Those contributions began in January 2011, and in February the church voted to borrow enough money to move forward with the work so the air conditioning would be complete by mid-June.

Overall, these improvements have made the building much more comfortable and useable.

The past decade has also seen more emphasis on direct mission involvement by church members. Previous direct action included mission trips to Honduras in the 1980s. Led by the Vickerys, the church has become most involved in mission projects in Ukraine and in Helena, Arkansas. Cooperative Baptist Fellowship (CBF) missionaries to Ukraine, the Podgaiskys, began ministering to homeless street children in Kiev. They saw the need for a special camp where children could be removed from the bad urban environment and grow up in a family setting. Jeffrey Vickery was part of a CBF group that located an abandoned children's camp at Bucha. An international Christian group bought the camp and began its renovation. The church sent members in 2004 and 2006 to help renovate this "Village of Hope." By 2007 foster families and street children began using the village, consisting in 2011 of a cafeteria, two cottages, and a dormitory.

The other main focus was on Helena, Arkansas, located in one of the poorest counties in the United States. Helping raise the standard of living and giving Christian hope there were special projects of CBF. Church members have traveled to Helena since 2005 to engage in community building projects. These have included teaching in a day camp, working in a community garden, renovating church and community buildings, constructing a pool house, and providing children's books and Bibles.

Another mission project has been fighting hunger. Recent studies have found that some fifty million people in the U. S. suffer from food insecurity. Some of these people are in Jackson County because of sustained high unemployment. The church has periodically collected food and other items for United Christian Ministries in Sylva (as well as giving it monetary support). Some members have also volunteered there. Starting in 2010 Jeffrey Vickery recognized that many children depended on free lunches in the public schools, lunches that were not available in the summer. So he organized church volunteers to distribute government-supplied food during the summer.

Cullowhee Baptist Church has also supported the planting of a new church. Jim Dean was given office space in the church building while he worked to organize the Summit Church. This group meets in the Cullowhee Valley School, but it hopes to construct its own building soon.

Within the past 20 years a series of events has caused Cullowhee Baptist Church to break longstanding ties with other Baptist organizations and form new relationships. These ties were broken because zealous conservatives (also called "fundamentalists") were determined to prevent anyone with moderate or liberal theological views from holding office in local, state, and national Baptist organizations. Until the 1970s Southern Baptists had tolerated a wide range of theological views in order to advance practical projects like seminaries, publishing houses, colleges, hospitals, and orphanages. Starting in 1979 conservatives began sharp electioneering practices in order to elect the presidents of the Southern Baptist Convention. They desired the election of men who believed in the inerrancy of the Bible. (Too many Baptist seminarians were questioning the creation stories, the virgin birth of Jesus, and his physical resurrection.) Conservatives reasoned that the election of conservative presidents for ten years would result in the presidents' appointments of various SBC boards that would employ only conservatives in SBC institutions. The test of conservatism was whether one believed that the Bible was factually correct and without error. This was a position that many moderate and liberal Baptists could not accept. Conservatives also opposed ordaining women as ministers. By 1990 the conservative revolution swept all moderates and liberals from positions of employment with the SBC. In corporate business terminology, it was a hostile takeover.

Cullowhee Baptist Church responded to this hostile takeover in various ways. In 1990 Pastor Joe Yelton proposed publishing in the Baptist press a resolution of the church. He wanted the Cullowhee church to resolve to seek peace within the SBC, "but not when it comes at the cost of lost convictions, silencing opposing viewpoints, and ethical determinations based upon majority votes." The church tabled this resolution, because it was not ready to sever ties with the SBC. Instead, the church established a denominational affairs committee to recommend a course of action. It voted to withhold funds from the state convention and the SBC until the committee recommended a course of action.

For months the committee, chaired by Pelham Thomas, collected information and attended meetings of moderates. One such meeting was held in Atlanta in 1990 and was attended by 3,000 delegates. It was the forerunner of the Cooperative Baptist Fellowship created in Atlanta in 1991 by 6,000 moderates. Cullowhee took the first step toward aligning with CBF in early 1991 by sending it $500, money that could have gone to the SBC.

About the same time the denominational affairs committee presented a report outlining the options for affiliation with Baptist groups. These options included staying in the SBC, becoming independent, joining the American Baptist Convention (also moderate), aligning with both the SBC and the ABC, joining the CBF, or joining the Southern Baptist Alliance, a more liberal group. The committee was clearly disappointed with the SBC over its recent actions. It had fired moderate seminary professors and editors, passed resolutions undermining the priesthood of the believer, published conservative Sunday School literature, and denied aid to new churches because they had women pastors. Yet the committee was unable to recommend one of the options it presented.

In 1992, however, the committee recommended affiliation with CBF. One action of the SBC clearly rankled the committee. In 1991 the SBC withheld funds from the Baptist seminary in Ruschlikon, Switzerland. This amounted to 40 percent of the budget. This was a seminary created in 1949 by the SBC to produce Baptist leaders for Europe. It was hoped that it would become a major center for educating Baptist leaders for Eastern Europe, an area being freed from Soviet control. The

SBC action was deemed deplorable because of the church's special connection to Ruschlikon. Keith Parker, a Jackson County native, was the foreign mission board's director of all SBC missionaries in Europe and a lecturer at Ruschlikon. He retired early rather than submit to the SBC requirement that missionaries subscribe to inerrancy. Thereupon the church agreed to send special Christmas and Easter offerings, which were usually designated for SBC missions, to Ruschlikon. This supplemented the support being given to Ruschlikon by CBF. The church then voted to break ties with the SBC, provided there was no adverse effect on the pastor's retirement fund. And there was none, so the ties were broken.

The affiliation with CBF placed Cullowhee Baptist Church squarely in the moderate camp. The major differences between CBF and the SBC were these: CBF rejected biblical inerrancy but the SBC used it as a test to determine who could hold office or be employed; furthermore, CBF believed the Bible should be interpreted in the light of Jesus' teachings; CBF was tolerant of diverse theological positions, whereas the SBC was not; the SBC owned and controlled institutions like seminaries, whereas CBF chose to affiliate with institutions that were sympathetic with its purposes; last, CBF supported women becoming ministers but the SBC did not.

The issue of women becoming ministers eventually caused the church to withdraw from the Tuckaseigee Baptist Association, an organization it had helped found in 1829. In 2002 Tonya and Jeffrey Vickery became co-pastors of the church. The association proposed to bar the church's messengers to the annual meeting because its hiring a woman minister was unbiblical. In addition, the 2000 SBC Faith and Mission statement (approved belatedly by the association executive committee) specified that "the office of pastor is limited to men as qualified by Scripture." Rather than wage a fight with the association, Cullowhee Baptist Church withdrew from the association before the annual meeting. Five other churches withdrew also, partly because they believed that every Baptist church was autonomous and could not have its policy dictated by another body. This controversy caused the church to strengthen its ties with other CBF churches in the area.

During the 1990s the North Carolina Baptist State Convention also came more under conservative control. The creation of CBF threatened to disrupt the convention. Rather than have CBF churches withdraw from the convention and thus decrease contributions to it, the convention allowed churches to designate whether their cooperative program monies should go to the SBC or CBF. Cullowhee Baptist Church specified that the convention send its portion of cooperative program monies to CBF. In 2008, however, the convention eliminated this provision. The church stopped contributions to the state convention and thus withdrew from it. Instead the church supported the state CBF organization.

From 1992 to 2008 the church broke all of its ties with the SBC, the Tuckaseigee Association, and the state convention. Yet the Baptist heritage and beliefs still resonate within the church because they had been established by centuries of custom and experience.

Stated succinctly, these beliefs are:

- The Bible is the authoritative guide in matters of faith and each person may interpret it as led by the Holy Spirit.
- The local church is self-ruling and no other organization may dictate to it.
- Each person serves as his or her own mediator with God.
- There are only two ordinances: baptism by immersion and communion.
- Every person has soul liberty to decide what religion to follow or not follow.
- Church and state should be separate.
- There are only two ordained officers: pastor and deacon.

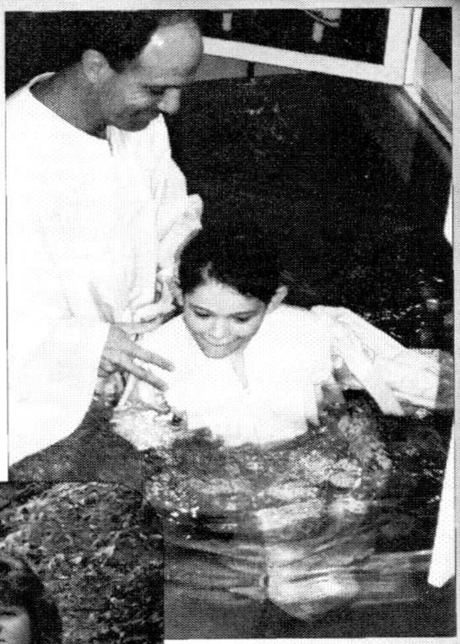

Pastor Mike Vanzura and Charles Holt, April, 1999

Pastor Jeffrey Vickery and Jill Ann Sutton Cook Standing Indian Campground, September, 2004

Pastor Tonya Vickery and Heather Ryan, October, 2011

Dr. John R. Bell, Jr.

Our author, John R. Bell, Jr., is professor of history emeritus at Western Carolina University in Cullowhee. He received his Ph.D. from the University of North Carolina at Chapel Hill. He has authored several books and articles.

A member of Cullowhee Baptist Church for many years, John has over the years researched and documented the history of the church on an ongoing basis. Along with his expertise in history, John has also had a keen interest in the history of the Baptist faith in North Carolina. His list of professional services is extensive:

■ Historical Committee, N. C. Baptist State Convention, 1965–1968, 1975–78

■ Historical Society of N. C.: R. D. W. Connor Award Committee, 1964

■ Social Sciences Consultant, Cherokee, N. C., High School, 1968–1969

■ North Carolina Literary and Historical Association offices: vice-president, 1970–1971, 1980–1981; executive committee, 1982–1985; president-elect, 1983–1984; president, 1984–1985

■ Co-organized the Biltmore House Symposium on Victorian Living and the Decorative Arts, April 22–24, 1981; Asheville, N.C.

■ Advisory Editorial Committee, *North Carolina Historical Review,* 1983–1988

■ Jackson County Committee to Celebrate the 400th Anniversary of the First Settlement in North Carolina, 1984–1986

■ Chairman, Jackson County Committee to Secure a County History, 1984–1987

■ Founding President, Jackson County Historical Association, 1985–1988, 1992–1993

■ Historical Society of North Carolina offices: Lefler Essay Award Committee, 1984–1985; Program Committee, 1986–1987; Chair of Committee on Relations Between Colleges and Schools, 1986–1988; president, 1996–1997

■ North Carolina Historical Highway Marker Advisory Committee, 1987-1992; 1993-1998

■ Reviewed Book Manuscripts: UNC Press, 1988, University of Tennessee Press, 1989

■ Reviewed Manuscripts for *Journal of Military History*, 1990s

■ Jackson County Historic Preservation Commission, 2009-2011

John and his wife, Dorothy Preslar Bell, have three children and four grandchildren.

Some History of
The Pastors of Cullowhee Baptist Church

The following information is as complete as the church records reflect, collected through the minutes of the church.

1822-1839—Adam Corn

Adam Corn, born in Virginia, was the son of a Revolutionary War soldier who was at Valley Forge. Adam moved to Wilkes County about 1794 and then settled in Buncombe County about 1808. Adam's mentor was Humphrey Posey who came to WNC as a missionary to the Cherokees in 1819. Posey came from the same part of Virginia as Corn. Adam began his ministry about 1820 at Crabtree Baptist Church. Debbie Corn Miranda, a descendant, tells us that Adam served chruches at Scotts Creek, Oconoluftee, Waynesville, Franklin, and Cowee, in addition to Cullowhee. Adam followed his mentor, Humphrey Posey, to Hiawassee, Georgia, where he remained until 1859, when his wife died. By 1860 Adam was back in Hendersonville, where he served churches at Ebenezer and Shooting Creek. He died in 1871. We do not have a photo of Adam Corn; however, we do have a photo of his son, Alfred Corn. *(Photo credit: Laura Mulcahy)*

Alfred Corn, son of Adam Corn, Born Jan 1817 in Cullowhee, *(then a part of Buncombe County, NC)*

1840—Bailey Kerby

1840, 1841, 1844, 1857—Thomas Henson

1852, 1869, 1883, 1884—William W. Reid

1854, 1858, 1863-1866, 1877—Joseph L. Buchanan

1855—McBickman? Rickman?

1856, 1857, 1872—William B. Crawford

1867—________Nelson

1868—William C. Berry

1868 William C. Berry

1874, 1876, 1890, 1891—Wilson Ensley

1878, 1879—Samuel C. Owens

1878, 1879 (another minister joined Owens)

1880, 1882, 1886, 1887—L. W. Hooper

1884, 1898—A. H. Sims

1874 Wilson Ensley

1891—A. C. Queen

1891—A. C. Queen

1888, 1889, 1893, 1899, 1901—Absalom Blythe Thomas

1896, 1903, 1904, 1906, 1908—T. F. Arrington

1897—G. A. Bartlett

1899—A. B. Smith

1901,1902—M. A. Love

1903—H. Davis

1908, 1909—W. B. Creasman

1909—W. T. Deitz

1910—P. T. McAfee

1910—J. T. Carson

1911—J. M. Bennett

1913—L. H. Crawford

1914, 1915, 1916—A. V. Joyner

1916—Edwin B. Harris

1919—John Hoglen

1922-1925—W. F. West

1925-1926—R. L. Randolph

1927-1935—I. K. Stafford

1910—P.T. McAfee

1913—L. H. Crawford

1910—J. T. Carson

1922-1925—W. F. West

1927-1935—Ivy Kenyon Stafford

1936-1941—Fred Forester

1942-1943—J. A. Herring

1943-1945—A. C. McCall

1945-1948—Mark R. Osborne, Jr.

1948-1952—Charles B. McConnell

1952—Francis Chesson, Interim Pastor

1952-1956—Roland Shaw Pruette

1956—Cloyes Starnes, Interim Pastor

1956-1962—Quentin M. Perreault

1962-1967—George Wilbur Braswell, Jr.

1936-1941—Fred Forester

1945-1948
Mark R. Osborne, Jr.

1948-1952
Charles B. McConnell

1952-1956
Roland Shaw Pruette

1956-1962
Quentin M. Perreault

1962-1967
George Wilbur Braswell, Jr.

1967
James S. Day
Interim Pastor

1968-1970—Lloyd Wood

1967—James S. Day, Interim Pastor

1968-1970—Lloyd Wood

1970-1973—Ted Purcell

1974—Page Lee, Interim Pastor

1974-1985—James Sydney (Jack) Hinson

1986—Earl Leininger, Interim Pastor

1986-1997—Joseph Yelton

1993-1997—Michael Dennis Vanzura, Associate Pastor

1997-1999—Michael Dennis Vanzura, Pastor

1999—Harold Anderson, Interim Pastor

2002-Present—Dr. Jeffrey & Tonya Vickery

1970-1973—Ted Purcell

1974-1985
James Sydney (Jack) Hinson

1986-1997—Joseph Yelton

1997-1999
Michael Dennis Vanzura

2002- Present
Dr. Jeffrey Vickery

2002- Present
Tonya Vickery

Some photos of ministers and their families

Reverend Wilson & Mary Ensley

June 1900 (front row): Irone Queen Coward, Rev. A.C. Queen, Ingsbo Wood Queen, Edgar Queen, Mary Jane Queen Hooper, Dora Hooper Hooper, John William Hooper, Flodia Hooper Coward; (back row): Theodore Queen and sisters

Reverend & Mrs. William West

Left: Reverend A.C. Queen selling Bibles

Reverend Fred & Ellen Forester

Reverend Charles B. McConnell, wife Ann McConnell with friend

Reverend Fred & Ellen Forester with sons: David, Stanley, James, Harry, Jonathan,

Reverend & Mrs. James S. Day, Jr.

Some photos of ministers and their families

Reverend Jack Hinson, Sara Hinson, and children Sarajane, Cydney, and Eric

Reverend Joseph & Corinne Yelton
Rosemary & Jake

Reverend Michael & Tracy Vanzura; Mia & Logan

Reverend Tonya & Dr. Jeffrey Vickery
Elizabeth & Ally

Cullowhee Baptist Church never had a full-time minister during the 1800s; he either pastored another church or farmed to supplement his existence. The minister was elected annually by the congregation with the option of being re-elected. In 1920, the church called its first full-time minister. The state convention paid a portion of his salary. It was not until 1962 that the church secured a full-time minister who was not supported, in part, by the state convention.

Some Messages from
Past Ministers of Cullowhee Baptist Church

GEORGE W. BRASWELL, JR., PASTOR 1962-1967

THE CALL

The pulpit committee heard me preach at the First Baptist Church of Canton in late July 1962 and invited me to preach at Cullowhee with a vote to follow the service. With segregation being challenged across our society and with their telling me that Cherokee Indian students and African Americans would be attending Western Carolina College and might attend the church services, what would be my position? I answered that if called I would expect a free pulpit. Joan and I had toured the old parsonage with the committee and saw an oil heater rusting in the yard and holes in the bedroom floors. The committee assured us of repairs and a source of heat. With an affirmative vote, Joan and I, with three-year-old Margaret Anne came to Cullowhee. On my first Sunday on Labor Day weekend 1962, chairs filled the aisles with members and students, including some Cherokees and African Americans. This new preacher fresh from Yale University Divinity School preached his heart out and the good mountaineers, of whom Joan was one, welcomed him for this new beginning.

THE MINISTRY

For years the church had a dual arrangement of the pastor serving also as chaplain to students, with financial support from the Baptist State Convention. Thus, I was the full-time pastor supported by the church financially with the convention naming and supporting a full-time chaplain. The church took a bold step in supporting a pastor full-time.

I relished the challenge of visiting every home possible up and down the river and in the valleys and on the mountain tops. Cullowhee was a classic "town and gown" community. We had deacons and deaconesses and Sunday School teachers who came from both community and campus work. I eagerly played basketball with college students at the campus gym. At the same time we engaged a hard working group of high school youth with exciting programs which eventually for several summers led the youth and adults to rent a house during the weeklong foreign mission week at Ridgecrest. Parents would bring vegetables and meats and do the cooking and chaperoning.

A vespers service and training union for all ages was a big thing on Sunday evenings, and Wednesday nights were for prayer service and committee meetings. Baptisms engaged us often and funerals too often with burial in the church cemetery.

I was known for my visitations of

dropping in at meal times and was always well received with great home cooking. One of the older members would say, "Here comes the little preacher." I was six feet tall and weighed all of 155 pounds. It was an affectionate term which he liked to share with others.

After Robbie was born in 1963 and Brien in 1964, the church made a big decision to build a parsonage; The old one with holes and cracks was torn down and the new brick house with full unfinished basement was built. Joan relished cooking meals for guests, for committees meeting at the parsonage, and for students and strangers.

Joan and I had considered foreign mission service back in earlier years. After living in the new house a little over two years, we were appointed by the Foreign Mission Board of the Southern Baptist Convention as its first missionaries to the country of Iran. We left Cullowhee with great gratitude and with deep sadness. The church had five years earlier called an untried pastor-to-be and had showered his family with love and generosity. The church had taken many risks in following the call of Jesus Christ in ministry and mission and in the summer of 1967 blessed one family of its own to go to the far corners of the earth.

SOME MARKERS AS I REMEMBER IN THE LIFE OF THE CHURCH

- Deeded land to the Baptist State Convention to build a Baptist Student Union building
- Assisted during the flooding of the river to get food and medicine to the stranded
- Prepared the Sunday service after the assassination of President Kennedy
- Living in a small two bedroom apartment while the new parsonage was built-the five of us
- Having two Southern Seminary professors all the way from Louisville to preach
- Studying at Union Theological Seminary in New York City on two week-long study leaves
- Having missionaries from Vietnam and Indonesia for weekend revivals
- Camping at Fontana Lake on youth retreats
- Welcoming summer visitors to the cool mountains who came for worship
- Exchanging choirs and pulpits with the black church in Asheville
- Having Dr. Paul Early, my former pastor, to preach a revival
- Putting windows up in the summer services to gain cool breezes
- Seeing diversity in the deacons' meetings with one wearing bibbed overalls and another wearing a bow tie
- Welcoming the pastor for meals and conversations in the homes
- Wishing to beat the Methodists to the cafeteria after Sunday worship
- Loving and accepting of each other after disagreements
- Bestowing love on Joan, Margaret Ann, Robbie, and Brien by so many
- Looking at the church with its background in the hills and valleys and being refreshed
- Preparing the final touches on the sermon with the echoes of the football game in the next door stadium
- Feeling the pains of separation after some five years of ministering together
- Having not a thought of ever leaving the wonderful life with Cullowhee Baptist Church and the community of Cullowhee for the city of Tehran, Iran, a city of five million Muslims
- Writing these words in 2011 bring back such fond memories of church folk and their families that I still feel a part of them

LLOYD WOOD,

PASTOR
1968-1970

MEMORIES

We came to Cullowhee in December of 1967 after graduating from Southern Seminary. We have many wonderful memories of our time there.

We were blessed to be welcomed to a church which offered open hearts and doors to the students of WCU, even minorities. Women were serving as deacons, a practice that was rare and still is in baptist churches. As we followed the church over the years, we saw the church continue to be a foward-looking and thoughtful people.

We adopted our daughter, Lori, in 1969. Our baby sitters were Lucile Painter and Percy and Gladys Parker, who often helped us out since we lived away from family. We kept up with them over the years, as well as with Baxter and Sue Wood who fed us almost every Sunday.

Some of our favorite memories involved our work with the youth group who met at our house on Sunday nights. We recall the trips to Ridgecrest and the camping trips to Stone Mountain Park, including a day trip to Six Flags. Mildred Norton accompanied us on several of these and served as cook.

There were so many other great people in the church, many who have passed on. We appreciate their friendship and support and are grateful for having spent a small part of our lives with them.

Loyd completed his pastoral ministry in the mid 1980s after serving churches for 25 years. He built and operated a childcare center until four years ago. Elaine began teaching music in the public schools retiring in 2002. We enjoy living near our daughter and two very loved grandchildren.

We wish you a wonderful day as you celebrate your heritage.

With fond memories,
Loyd and Elaine Wood

TED PURCELL,
PASTOR
1970-1974

MEMORIES AND REFLECTIONS

On this occasion, when this church celebrates her 190th anniversary, it is natural for me to recall that I was there during the Sesquicentennial (150th). I remember that it was a time of great excitement and interest as many people helped bring to life the history and ministry of Cullowhee Baptist Church.

I remember with gratitude the community outreach of what some called a "town and gown" congregation, committed to a ministry to and with a diverse group that included university faculty, staff, and students as well as other local people with deep historic roots in the surrounding area. It was in the context of this unique ministry that I discerned a call to campus ministry that later led me to N.C. State (1974-1989) and Duke University (1989-2011).

The limitations of space and my memory prevent me from responding more fully to this invitation to recall and write. But the beauty of my time with you is yet with me, and includes many faces of friendship, experiences of pastoral companionship during joys and sorrows, times of hospitality with my family, sharing the hard work of learning to live and speak the truth in love to one another and to the world that hungers for God. I feel deeply honored to have been one of the pastors of Cullowhee Baptist Church. This church made significant contributions to my spiritual formation and growth.

I give thanks to God as I celebrate with you the 190 years of ministry, and carry within my heart this graceful reminder of how we all are part of the ongoing story of God.

Grace, peace, and thanksgiving,
Ted Purcell

JACK HINSON, PASTOR 1974-1985

HIGHLIGHTS

Cullowhee Baptist Church occupies a precious place in my museum of memories. Beginning with my ministry there on August 1, 1974, I felt a strong sense of the calling of the Lord that continued until my resignation in 1985.

When the university opened the fall semester each year extra chairs were placed in the aisle to accommodate the students in morning worship. Fraternities came in groups as part of their induction ceremonies. Athletes and coaches were present, often after a long bus trip from a distant city. Before the days of drums and guitars were common in church, the WCU Jazz Band slipped into the sanctuary one Sunday (at my request). The congregation clapped and tapped to a jazzy version of "Amazing Grace."

International students generated a holiday atmosphere in the services. Church families provided a home away from home through the Student Adoption Plan. The Festival of Faith brought noted preachers to the church and the university each autumn.

High School students from all over the community met on Sunday evening for Bible study and fun. They took the long trip to the Baptist Assembly at Caswell each summer.

The Women's Missionary Union kept mission fires aglow throughout the year. Extra energy was given to the Annie Armstrong Easter offering and the Lottie Moon Christmas offering.

WCU had no formal counseling service. Unsettled students found their way to my office. There were no Wednesday evening activities, only a Tuesday night church business meeting once a quarter. About three years into my ministry a need was brought to my attention for a Wednesday prayer service. It started with a small group, sharing and praying together.

As far as I know, the practice of joining hands for prayer at the close of Sunday worship was first introduced to the church family and warmly accepted.

Visiting shut-ins or just dropping by the homes of members furnished great blessings to me. During the Christmas season I called on young people who were home from college or military service.

In 1977 morning worship moved downstairs for a brief time while new carpet and new chandeliers were installed in the sanctuary. The floor was also refinished along with the pews.

Another organ was purchased in 1979. Also, Royal Ambassadors and Children's Church were created.

In 1983 I began praying daily for the Lord to send us a project big enough to challenge us. My prayer was answered in 1985, when through God's grace, He multiplied the request and answered the prayer with not one, but a list of projects:

* The Properties Committee led a campaign to refurbish the building. A specialist was called in from the Baptist State Convention. Committees were formed. A time table was set to raise funds. The congregation pledged $68,000.
• The Vision Committee worked through the process of writing a new church covenant.
• The Wednesday night prayer group grew into a family night supper and fellowship time. WCU students attended without charge.
• The youth group proposed a Youth Week and a Planned Famine.
• Offerings and tithes exceeded budget requirements. In addition $2500.00 was raised through a church-wide campaign for world hunger relief that included prayer and fasting.
• New hymnals were purchased.
• A softball team was organized.
• A handbell choir was established.
• A Passover–Communion meal took place during Lent.

I never perceived what some college churches describe as "a town and gown" distraction. University personnel along with people from every segment of the community combined hearts and minds in a creative, diverse partnership for worship and service in the Kingdom.

I am grateful for the privilege of serving as pastor of Cullowhee Baptist Church.

Jack Hinson

JOSEPH YELTON, PASTOR

1986–1997

PRECIOUS MEMORIES!

In August of 1986, my wife Corinne and I rolled into Cullowhee for the very first time as Pastor Team of Cullowhee Baptist Church. Accompanied by our two-year-old daughter Rosemary and our six-month-old son Jacob, we were greeted at the Old Cullowhee Road parsonage by a small army of members who were ready to unload our truck and help us spend our first Cullowhee night in our very own beds. We did. In no small part, our presence at Cullowhee Baptist at this particular time and place was due to a relationship I had developed as a college student (1973–77) with Harry and Sue Duke. These magnificent people absorbed me into their home because of the church "Adopt-a-Student" ministry. I, along with five "brothers and sisters" would go to Harry and Sue's

Sunday evening, together eating pizza and watching "60 Minutes" on CBS. Because of the richness of that relationship, which stands to this day, when Cullowhee Baptist was looking for a pastor to follow the Reverend Jack Hinson (who was my college pastor as well as a member of my ordaining Presbytery at First Baptist of Asheville), they came to Virginia and visited with my family.

With so much investment in my life by the good people of Cullowhee early on, I was eager to begin a ministry that would end up stretching from 1986 to 1997. Yes, it was a little intimidating to come back and become pastor to former professors like Drs. Polly and Jerry Rice, Jack Barnett, Dr. James Dooley, and more. In no time, they had calmed my concerns and received kindly my best (but often lacking) efforts as pastor.

New ministries to trailer parks, Honduras, and the like joined hands with ecumenical efforts that allowed Cullowhee to become one of the five charter founders of Jackson County United Christian Ministry.

I remember the Sunday morning I baptized into the Cullowhee fellowship Mr. Jarvis Graham, a WCU senior. I stand 5'10" while Jarvis, a forward for Western's basketball team stood 7'4". It was like laying down a Redwood. We all laughed and celebrated as Cullowhee Baptist, for the first time, in a long time became an
officially integrated church.

Many of my bungles as pastor were all too obvious, but some of them were well covered by people like Etheree Chancellor, the Lovedahls, the Younts, the Dooleys, the Baxleys, and the Searcys. I could go on and on. They and many others took good care of me and mine. To this day I receive lots of wonderful phone calls from my dear friend, Robert Lanning. To one and all, I miss and appreciate you.

There were hard days, too. We continued attending Southern Baptist Convention meetings but could only watch as that once-mighty bastion of cooperation became another casualty of narrow doctrinal fundamentalism. Cullowhee Baptist became the first North Carolina congregation to officially leave the Southern Baptist Convention because of this rift. I believe the year was 1993.

Most of what we experienced together was magnificent. Fondly I recall, and will continue to recall, the Christmas bonfires at the Yelton home on top of the mountain. Babies were born, graduations attended to, funerals endured and marriages celebrated. Cullowhee Baptist provided the full package of quality Christian ministry.

I suppose the greatest memory I hold (nostalgia may have occluded it a bit) is with the beautiful college students of Western Carolina University. It was amazing watching the sanctuary go from half-full to overflowing in a two-week period of time as August would abruptly end summer and usher in wide-eyed students. It was wonderful and amazing, and to this day I cherish and celebrate dozens of former student relationships that have blossomed into something new.

Most of all, I think of Cullowhee Baptist as a cherished church who literally impacted the world by taking care of students from Asia, Europe, Africa, Australia, and both of the Americas.

Cullowhee Baptist sent lots of people back to their homes with a warm and enduring "American" experience. They did precisely the same for every student who gave them the chance, whether from North Carolina or the outer reaches of the other forty-nine states.

You, dear Cullowhee Baptist Church, change people every day. You changed me. For you I am both indebted and grateful. You are loved.

Joe Yelton

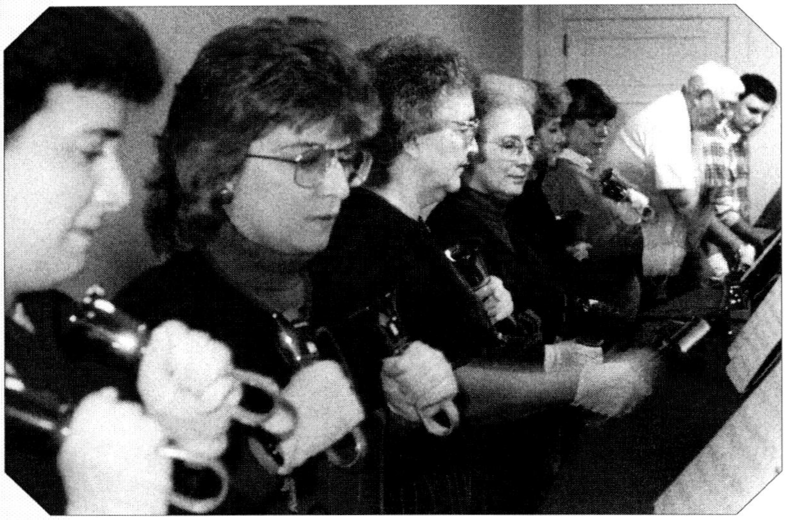

1991Bell Choir: college student, Beth Baxley, Barbara Dooley, Mary Helderman, Frances Conley, Sandy Davis, Jack Barnett, Jeff Davis

Some History of
Our Church Buildings and Locations

by John Bell, with selections by Amy Ammons Garza

The first church meeting was held in a log structure near the confluence of Love's Branch and the Tuckaseigee River at Webster, NC. The church moved in 1830, to a hewn-log building near the mouth of Cullowhee Creek. (E. H. Stillwell's "Historical Sketch of Tuckaseegee Baptist Association" (1829-1929) states: ". . .the chruch was moved to a site near the mouth of Cullowhee Creek where a small log house served as a place of worship. This log structure stood directly in front of where R. V. Brown now has a stock of goods at Cullowhee." The store known as Brown's Store was located where Kindermusik is today.)

The Tuckaseigee's periodic flooding chased the people to higher ground; and in 1856, a church building was constructed on property adjacent to the present church cemetery. Other structures–frame buildings–were constructed on the periphery of the cemetery in 1885, and then again in 1918. The present brick building was completed in 1929. *(Since we have no pictures of the first four buildings, those depicted in the illustration on the following page are sketches of what the buildings of the day might have looked like.)*

In the 1880s, services were held one weekend out of the month–on Saturday for business and on Sunday for worship. Not until the early 1900s did the church hold weekly Sunday worship services. In the 1820s there was no educational program; however, by 1890, the Sunday School Program had become a regular agency for teaching the Bible.

The first Vacation Bible School was held in 1928 and has since come to be recognized as an important part of Christian education.

The late 1800s witnessed other changes. The church organized an effective Sunday school, emphasized educated ministers, supported missionaries to the Cherokees, and started the Women's Missionary Union for the support of missions. This union provided leadership training for women and led to changes in the Tuckaseigee Association. At first only men could serve as messengers from the churches to the association, but by 1920 women became messengers.

Other changes occurred in the 1900s. Up to 1929 the church had built four successive buildings, none of them adequate. Then the state convention granted part of the money needed to build the present church building. The congregation lacked the funds necessary to meet the needs of ministering to students, so the convention considered its funding of the building to be a missionary activity. Likewise, the church could not afford a full-time minister until the state convention agreed to pay half the salary of one in the 1920s. It was understood that the minister would spend half of his time ministering to students. This arrangement continued until 1962, when the church fully paid the minister and the convention employed a full-time director of the Baptist Student Union. The director soon had a BSU building constructed on land leased from the church.

While at Webster, the Church was called Unity Baptist; it was renamed Cullowhee Baptist Church upon moving to Cullowhee Creek.

Illustration by Doreyl Ammons Cain

With the church now located in Cullowhee, the church grew as the area around it began to change, with its focus on education. The following is a history of how a public school became Western Carolina University.

In 1888, citizens of Cullowhee who desired a better school for the community than was

Fifth Church Building 1918-1929

Scene on Cullowhee State Normal Campus, Mid-1920s

offered in public schools of that day organized a board of trustees and established a community school known as Cullowhee Academy.

Founded in August 1889 as a semi-public secondary school and chartered as Cullowhee High School in 1891 (also called Cullowhee Academy), it served the Cullowhee community and boarding students from neighboring counties and other states.

The founder, Robert Lee Madison, wanted to provide an education for the young people in the region and train teachers to spread education throughout the western part of the state.

1928—view from Buzzard's Roost, comprising what then was the entire campus of Cullowhee State Normal School. Seen here are CBC, Madison Building, old heating plant, Davies Home, the Music and Art Building; Joyner Building, Moore Dormitory in progress and the Cullowhee Methodist Church.

Closeup 1924

Closeup 1928

Sixth Church Building 1929-Current

In 1893, through the efforts of Walter E. Moore, representative from Jackson County, the North Carolina Legislature authorized an appropriation for the establishment of a normal department at the school "for the purpose of training teachers." This designation became the first publicly funded normal school in North Carolina.

In 1905, the state assumed title to the school's buildings and property and made it a state institution. That same year, the school's name was changed to Cullowhee Normal and Industrial School. In 1925, the school's name was changed to Cullowhee State Normal School. Cullowhee Normal trained over 2000 teachers by the mid-1920s.

1940s—Campus is now called Western Carolina Teachers College Campus

1970s

Over the next 40 years, the school expanded its curriculum and evolved into a junior college, and in 1929 it was chartered by the legislature as a four-year institution under the name Western Carolina Teachers College. Called "the Cullowhee experiment," Madison's idea became a model for the other regional colleges in the state. The demand for both liberal arts and other programs led to an expansion of the school's offerings. Postgraduate studies and the Master of Arts in Education degree were added to the curriculum in 1951. In 1953, the name "Western Carolina College" was adopted. In 1967, the institution was designated a regional university and given its current title, "Western Carolina University." On July 1, 1972, WCU became a member of the University of North Carolina system.

November 17, 1997

Cullowhee Baptist Church 2011
on the Western Carolina University Campus

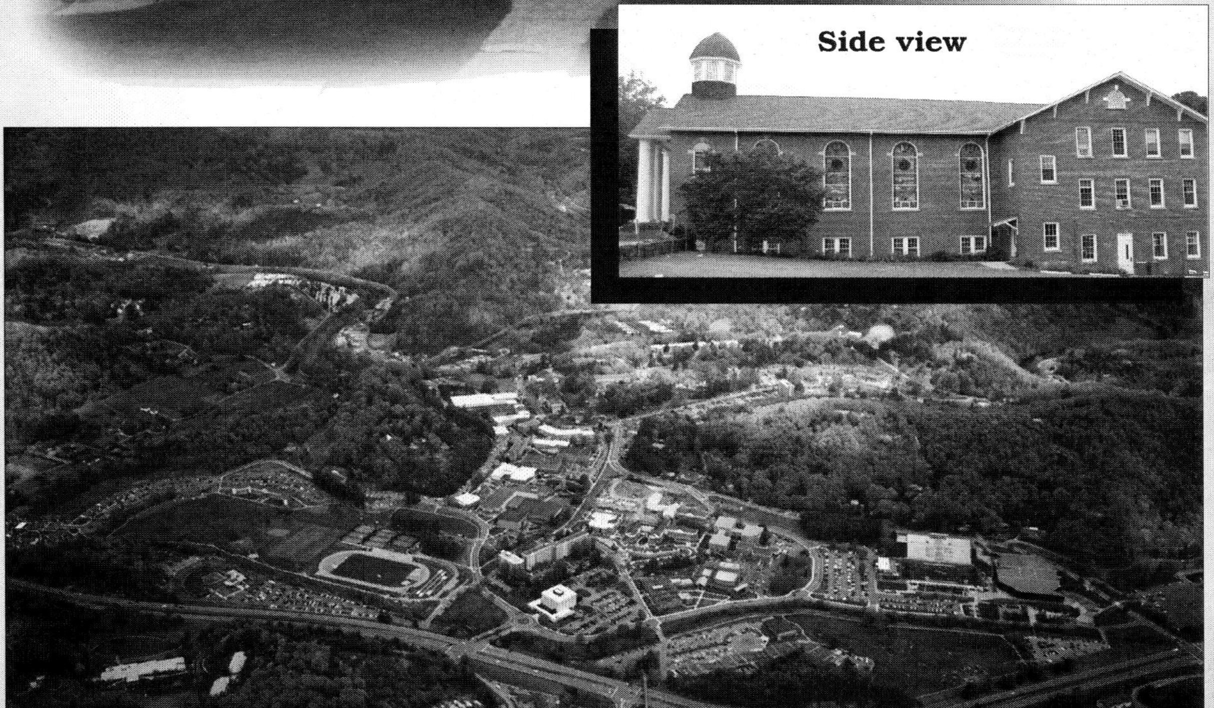

Side view

Some History of Becoming

Mother Church to Many Community Baptist Churches

by John Bell, with selections by Amy Ammons Garza

As mentioned before, one of the reasons for the slow growth of Cullowhee Baptist Church was the creation of new churches. Members came from a wide area, and travel was difficult. The early members lived the length of the Tuckaseigee and Oconoluftee river valleys. The 1979 *Report of the Historical Committee Tuckaseigee Baptist Association* lists the following: "During the first 50 years of its history records show that Cullowhee Baptist Church helped to organize many other churches in nearby neighborhoods, among which were Scotts Creek, Savannah, Caney Fork, Oconalufty, Tuckaseigee, Speedwell and Little Savannah." It also states, "The following persons were ordained to preach by the Cullowhee Baptist Church: Thomas Henson, Joseph Buchanan, Benjamin Hatfield, Bailey Kerby, T.C. Buchanan, Wilson Ensley, W.B. Crawford, B.S. Queen, L.W. Hooper and J.D. Sitton."

After the Civil War, the blacks from Cullowhee also formed their own church, **Webster Black Baptist Church,** which no longer stands.

In 1828 some 34 members left to form the "Ochonia Luftia" church. The building itself, built in 1912, became the **Oconaluftee Baptist Church** (Smokemont Baptist Church) and is now a historic church in Cherokee, North Carolina. The building was added to the National Register in 1976.

On March 26, 1830 the **Scotts Creek Baptist Church** was organized, under the guidance of Rev. Humphrey Posey. Posey, Adam Corn, and Stephen White were known for establishing churches in Western North Carolina. The first church building was a small log house erected near a wagon road on Hatfield land. The church was organized with 12 charter members who were released from Cullowhee Baptist Church. These charter members were Daniel Bryson, Thomas Woodfin, Thomas Styles, Lakey Elliott, Benjamin Hatfield, Susannah Hatfield, Mary Underwood, Mary Mull, Martha Hatfield, Lucy Stiles, Catherine Davis and Artie Bryson. Soon thereafter J. Stiles, Daniel Woodfin, Jane Styles, Mary Stiles, Margaret Kerklin, Lavinia Patterson, and Mary A. Mull were released from Cullowhee to join the Scotts Creek Church. These names are listed among the list of messengers from Scotts Creek to the Tuckaseigee Baptist Association in 1830.

In 1836 the Parkers, Hoopers, Catheys. Websters, and Cowards withdrew to form a new church at Caney Fork. The congregration of **Caney Fork Baptist Church**, originally constituted on December 17, 1836, was located in East La Porte. This church eventually evolved into the **Tuckasegee Baptist Church**, located just off Highway 107 in Tuckasegee, N.C. Other congregrations came from this church, i.e.: in 1846 came the Hamburg arm of the Caney Fork Baptist Church; in 1859, the Baptist Church at Caney Fork granted letters of dismissal to 16 members, in order that they might constitute a church at John's Creek; and in 1882, "on motion granted a letter of dismission to Brother Baxter Hooper and Sister Lou Long to unite with other churches at East Laport the 3rd Sunday in May"--and this church has evolved into the East LaPorte's Grace Community Church.

Old Savannah Baptist (circa 1836), is located just outside of historical Dillsboro in Jackson County. **Speedwell Baptist** (circa 1902), now called Speedwell Missionary Baptist Church, is located on Speedwell Baptist Road in Cullowhee, N.C. **Little Savannah Baptist Church** (circa 1914), is located on Little Savannah Road in Cullowhee, N.C.

Excerpt from the original minutes:

1830

16 Jan 1830 Church met and ordained Brother Hatfield to the ministry. Dismissed the following members [to form Scotts Creek Baptist Church]: J. Stiles, T. Stiles, ?? Elett(?), B. E. Hatfield, Thos, Woodfin, Daniel Woodfin, Daniel Bryson, Susannah Hatfield Jane Stiles, Martha Hatfield, Lucinda Stiles, Katharine Davis, Mary Stiles, Arty Bryson, Mary Long, Mary Underwood, Margaret Kerklin, Lavina Patterson, Mary A. Mull.

October 25, 1902

Letters issued to the following "to organize a church at Speedwell": L. E. Adams, Articia Mathis, Dana (or Dora) Mathis, Elbert Mathis, Hix Ashe, dtr of Cling Ashe, John Mathis, Julia Mathis (Mrs. M. W.?), M. W. Mathis, C. G. Boone, Riley Morrison, A. J. Presley, C. L. Presley, D. S. Presley (or Pressley), Daniel Boone, Margaret Parker, H. D. Presley, Jake Presley, L. C. Presley, C. E. Dills, Lula Presley, Elijah (W. E.?) Seago, Belle Stiles, Penny (or Perry) Coggins, ???? Watson, Z. V. Watson, Ermie (?) Wilson, J. R. Dills, T. C. Wilson, Ida Fox, Mary Fox, Nellie Hooper, R. E. Hooper, Richard Hooper, W. A. Hooper.

April ??, 1914

To organize Little Savannah church: Bertie Bishop, Bessie Bishop, Grover Bishop, Mattie Bishop, Neal Bishop, Belle Brown, Mack Brown, Cassie or Corsie Hooper, Oscar Lewis.

Another church that called Cullowhee Baptist Church its "home church," is **Black Mountain Baptist Church** (circa 1919) in the Wayehutta Community of Cullowhee, located near the site of the present-day church.

Black Mountain Baptist Church was officially organized in 1919. However, historical records, remembrances of community people and others indicate that the church actually began in the Wayehutta Community long before 1919, when people from Cullowhee Baptist Church and other churchs released members to organize the chruch.

Rev. John Sitton was the first preacher, as indicated by records, community members, and other people. The first services were held under a tree before or during 1885. The first building was a workshop owned by Columbus Bryson around 1896. This building was located on the bank of Wayehutta Creek. The sound of the water was so loud it was hard to hear the speaker. During this period, Iva Bryson Dills was on her way one day to bring the cows home to milk. She was very concerned about the Christian welfare of the young folks in the community. Rev. Sitton happened to be approaching her from the opposite end of the road. From their conversation that day, Rev. Sitton and Mrs. Dills made plans for Iva to talk with people at the lower end of the community and Rev. Sitton with people at the upper end. A meeting of the community folks evolved. At this meeting, $25.00 was collected to buy materials to start the first building. It was constructed of logs around 1910,

---

Excerpt from the original minutes:
(Minutes Book 1885-1899)

Nov. 26, 1899, p. 84 Weary-Hutta School House

J. D. Sitton began a series of meetings at Weary-Hutta School House and continued until the 28th, then was assisted by Rev. A. Norman.
The doors of Cullowhee Church was opened Dec. 2nd by J. D. Sitton. Sister Julia Bryson joined by experience. Rev. T. F. Arrington entered the services and assisted by preaching Dec. 4th. The doors of the Cullowhee Church was opened Dec. 7th. Joined by experience Bro. John Bryson and Lucius Deitz. Doors of church opened Dec. 8th. Joined by experience Joel Cabe, Mary Cabe, and Allie A. Bryson. Dec. 9th Mary Nicholson and Mary Mills joined by experience.
Dec. 9th, 1899, Rev. T. F. Arrington baptised the following candidates: Joel Cabe, Lucius Deitz, John Bryson, Mary Cabe, Maggie Mills, Mary Nicholson, Julia Bryson, and Annie Bryson.
Signed by G. E. Painter, Supt. of Weary-Huitta Sunday School.

May 7, 1919

"Of constituting a Missionary Baptrist Church at Wayehutta" Artie Bryson, Columbus Bryson, Sina Dean, Emma Dills, Julia Dills, Iva Dills

---

Black Webster Baptist Church
Photo taken in 1982. Church destroyed by fire shortly thereafter.
(Photo Credit: Victoria Casey McDonald)

Organized 1828-Built in 1912 Oconaluftee Baptist Church—Smokemont, NC

Organized 1830
Scotts Creek Baptist Church
Sylva, N.C.

Organized 1836
Old Savannah Baptist Church
Sylva, N.C.

Organized 1836 as Caney Fork
1892 Original Tuckasegee Baptist Church
Tuckasegee, N.C.
(Photo Credit: Mary Jo Hooper Cobb)

Built 1902
Speedwell Missionary Baptist Church
Cullowhee, N.C.

Organized 1914
Little Savannah Baptist Church
Cullowhee, N.C.

Organized 1919
Black Mountain Baptist Church
Cullowhee, N.C.

Some History of
MUSIC AND CHOIRS AT CULLOWHEE BAPTIST CHURCH

by Barbara and James Dooley

Cullowhee Baptist Church was organized some 30 years before Jackson County was officially established and less than two generations after the American Revolution. Communication, transportation, and commerce were still in early stages of development, and most community organizations would necessarily have been relatively simple in structure and function. Numerous white settlements had been established in the region during this period, but many Cherokee Indians also remained in the area. Serving several communities that were in formative stages, the church would certainly be considered a pioneer congregation.

During the colonial era and in the decades leading up to Cullowhee Baptist Church's founding, many small-town and rural churches regarded music as essential to their religious experience. They sang Psalms and hymn texts (in metrical settings) to tunes brought with them from Europe. One of the most well known brought to America by colonists was *Old Hundredth* (Doxology)–the familiar Psalm text and tune which is still sung centuries later. In time, Americans began composing new hymn texts and tunes, and congregational singing flourished, enriched with the expanded repertory.

When music instruction was provided, particularlyteaching church members to read music notation, it was usually based on the very old solmization syllables: *fa, sol, and la* (which, when repeated and extended with "*mi,*" form the major scale: *fa, sol, la, fa, sol, la, mi, fa.*

These same churches also would have been adding hymns to their services from the growing body of newly composed texts and tunes by American poets and composers. By the beginning of the 19th century, the solmization system, commonly called "*fa-so-la,*" became even more popular with the introduction of unique shapes for note heads representing the different pitches of the scale–a visual aid for reading music. Hence the term, "Shape Note Singing," for a style and repertory which today is practiced (in numerous versions and collections) by enthusiasts throughout the country.

Although these collections enjoyed widespread acceptance and use in rural churches of the South, if singing schools were organized and conducted in Cullowhee Baptist Church, records and recollection of those activities have been lost.

Music in the spread of "Shape Note Singing" is not to be confused with or considered the same as "Gospel Music" which, beginning in the southeast during the early 20th century, has enjoyed widespread popularity. The musical style of gospel music is significantly different from that of the shape note singing, and the performance practices contrast dramatically. The rise of gospel music, while significant for many churches and denominations, seems never to have been a factor in the history of Cullowhee Baptist Church where a more traditional style of worship service was obviously practiced.

A significant development in many churches was the appointment of music teachers/leaders whose responsibility was to guide congregations in their commitment to learning and singing appropriate music in their services. Of special note in the church minutes of April, 1890, is Cullowhee Baptist Church's appointment of Samuel W. Henson as "Singing Cleark (sic) for 12 months."

There is no mention of musical instruments in the early records of the Cullowhee church, but the music leaders may have used tuning forks, which were relatively common during that period. However, the church obviously purchased a (pedal) pump organ at some point during the early years of the 20th century, because there is a February 15, 1912, note in the church's minutes reporting that a balance of $8.28 was owed on the church organ. The organ was built by the Cornish Organ Co. in Washington, New Jersey. Much later, the church minutes for July 7, 1929, indicate that the instrument was to be loaned to Prof. J.S. Seymour for use of the Men's Class in the boiler room. The church still possesses what is believed to be this same organ; it has been restored to good condition and is used for special programs.

The founding of Western Carolina University near the turn of the 20th century likely exerted significant influence on the worship style and music of both Cullowhee Baptist Church and Cullowhee Methodist Church, located as they are on the university campus. The arts, including music, were an important emphasis in the school's curriculum, and it is not unreasonable to assume that faculty and students would have valued the historic roots of church music and its power to instill joy, majesty, solemnity, humility, and reverence in worship services—religious values characteristic of Cullowhee Baptist. It is not surprising to find consistent references to time-honored hymns such as the traditional Doxology, "All Hail the Power of Jesus' Name," and "Holy, Holy, Holy," listed in the records of worship services. The first hymn to be identified by name in the church minutes is a hymn of this type. On March 23, 1901, the congregation sang "Am I a Soldier of the Cross" during the invitation to membership. They continued to sing while the right hand of fellowship was extended to the new members.

The second reference found in church minutes regarding music leadership is dated 13 June, 1920, and reports that choir leader, Rufus D. Phillips, and organist, Mrs. F. L. Wells, were elected by the congregation. This entry also mentions that the organist and choir leader were to recommend a song book for purchase (title not given).

In January, 1929, the church paid $68 for 110 copies of the *Modern Hymnal* (published in 1926), which comprised a broad collection of standard hymns as well as newer hymns included for popular appeal.

"Special music" is first mentioned in the church minutes in 1930. This terminology was common among Southern Baptist Churches and typically indicated that a choir, ensemble, or soloist(s) would perform the music selections.

The church periodically held special observances. "Revival" services were the most common, and guest singer/song leaders often were engaged for these services. The July 7, 1931, minutes reported that "Mr. W. Furman Betts was paid $51.08 plus $18 for travel expense for leading the singing in a recent revival at the church." Church attendance must have been increasing during the early 1930s because by September of 1935, still more hymnals were needed, and the pastor was charged with locating and purchasing the required number.

Beginning in December 1943, an exceptionally active Cullowhee Baptist Church choir program was organized under the leadership of Professor H. P. Smith, director, and his wife, Zula, who served as accompanist. Dr. Smith was a professor in social studies at Western Carolina Teachers College, and his background obviously included education and experience in music. The church's adult choir was expanded by recruiting numerous college students, and the combined group was given the name of Chapel Choir during this period. The music program also expanded to include (1) a Junior Choir of 39 members, directed by Jack Barnett, a member of the church and the college faculty; and (2) a Youth Choir of 14 members, directed by Carl Painter. The choir loft was refurbished, and a social room was arranged for the choir.

From the outset, a repeated commitment of participants in the music program beyond their leadership role in the church's regular Sunday morning and evening services, was to nurture a "love and respect for good church music."

The choir presented numerous formal concerts, including cantatas appropriate for Christmas and Easter celebrations, portions of Handel's *Messiah,* and programs composed of various titles of sacred music. During the following 12 years, scores, if not hundreds, of college students sang in the group, and it was common to have as many as 70 to 75 singers involved in their performances. The music programming often included selections performed by soloists and smaller ensembles formed from the membership.

During 1945, the choir organized and launched a fundraising program to purchase a Hammond electronic organ that would serve as a memorial, paying tribute to members of the U. S. armed forces who had lost their lives in World War II. By May of 1946, their goal was reached, and the new organ was purchased and installed. Dedicatory services were conducted in the church sanctuary on the first Sunday in May. Dr. H. T. Hunter, president of the college and active member of the congregation, accepted the organ for the church. The

Some Photos of Choirs Past and Present

1940s

Center: H.P. Smith, choir director, and his wife, Mrs. Zula Smith, organist; Christmas, 1940s

1950s

1970s

pastor, the Reverend Mark Osborne, Jr., preached the dedicatory sermon in the morning service, and Mrs. H. P.Smith served as organist. Guest organist, George Thompson of Asheville, and the church choir presented a dedicatory concert of sacred music in the evening service.

In 1946, as the choir matured in size and ability, the group organized and initiated several concert tours, eventually traveling to Asheville, Bryson City, Canton, Drexel, Hendersonville, Mars Hill, Morganton, Murphy, Webster, and as far east as Greenville, S.C., to present a total of 25 concerts.

During the 1950-51 school year, the choir's founder-director resigned. The college was creating a graduate studies division, and Smith was a key faculty member involved in the process. It is presumed that he determined his schedule would not allow him to continue the same investment of time and attention he had given the music program. Both Dr.Richard Renfro and Clayton Curtis, music department faculty members at Western, are cited in the *Sylva Herald* as having directed the choir in concerts during this period, but Smith was able to resume his leadership in time for the 1952 Christmas concert.

Jame and Barbara Dooley, daughters Gail and Claire, 1970s

In December 1953, the choir organized a successful fundraiser to purchase chimes for the Hammond organ. The chimes were presented and dedicated October 16, 1955.

Director H. P. Smith retired from the director's position in 1955 and became advisor to the group. Leadership of the Chapel Choir passed to a series of individuals, including long-time choir and church member Jack Barnett, and the group continued its regular service to the congregation and community. Succeeding generations of leadership have maintained that same commitment.

More recently, in 1979, handbells were introduced as an instrumental resource, enhancing worship services on many occasions. In 1996, the music program initiated a choir scholar program, providing scholarships to university vocal students who sing in the adult choir. Student instrumentalists from the university are frequently engaged to provide a solo performance or to enhance the organ/piano choir accompaniment in church services.

The musically talented and dedicated church musicians at Cullowhee Baptist Church, amateurs and professionals alike, continue to maintain their devotion to "good church music," a time honored commitment as a heritage passed through all the generations from 1821 to the present.

1970s (continued)

Pamela Richardson, pianist in 1976

1980s

1990s

Cullowhee Baptist Church Choir Directors

1890-1891	S. W. Henson, appointed for twelve months as Singing Cleark {sic}
1920	Rufus D. Phillips
1935	Mrs. Gulley
1935	C. F. Dodson, assistant
1942	Mrs. J. A. Herring
1943-1951	Hugh Preston Smith
1943	Sara Jones, assistant
1948-1949	Jack Barnett, Junior Choir; Carl Painter, Youth Choir
1949	Wanda Joan Rogers, Junior Choir
1949-1951	Ruth Hooper, Youth Choir
1951	Richard Renfro
1951-1952	Clayton Curtis
1952-1956	Hugh Preston Smith
1956	Arnold Penland, Jr.
1956	Mrs. Clayton Croom, Youth Choir
1956	Eucella Hamilton, Junior-Intermediate Choir
1956	Laysel Bancroft
1956	Barbara Shaver, assistant
1957	Jack Barnett
1958	Vanita Croom
1958-1968	Edgar vom Lehn
1959	Barbara Fowler, Junior Choir
1959	Eucella Hamilton, Youth Choir
1959	Revé Perreault, Youth Choir.
1962	Stanton H. Procter, Junior Choir
1962	Mrs. Joe Barnhart, Youth Choir
1964	Kohlan Flynn, Youth Choir
1969-1970	Earl Owen
1970-1971	Temple Smith, interim
1971	Dianne Hooper, Youth Choir
1971-1975	Joyce Farwell
1973-1975	Joyce Farwell, Children's Choir
1975-1983	Sara Hinson, Adult and Youth Choirs
1983-1984	Ron Caldwell
1984-1985	Tim Stiles, interim
1985-1986	Sara Hinson, interim
1986-1992	Corinne Yelton, Adult and Youth Choirs
1992-1996	Ann Lough, interim
1996	Sara Hinson, interim
1996-1998	James Dooley
1998	Steve Baxley, interim
1999-2001	Terri Ducker
2001	Steve Baxley, interim
2003-Present	Steve Baxley

2002

2011

Donny Gibson, Organist

Barbara Dooley, Pianist

Steve Baxley, Minister of Music

Some History of Our Missions

Missions Give Purpose to Life

by Irene Bishop Hooper

What do you think of when you see or hear the word missions? Many faces and places fill my mind. The new *Webster's Dictionary* (revised 1992) defines the word mission as "a group of people sent (especially abroad) by a church or other religious organizations to make conversions". A second definition is "an aim in life arising from a conviction or a sense of calling."

For the Christian, the word "missions" gives purpose to life. Jesus Christ is the Captain of our soul. His commands to His followers were: "Therefore, go and make disciples of all nations, baptizing them in the name of the Father and of the Son and of the Holy Spirit, and teach them to obey everything I have commanded you. And sure, I am with you always, to the very end of the age" (Matthew 28:19, 20).

When we accept Christ as our Lord and Savior, we commit ourselves to His service. My mind scans the centuries past as His followers have tread through toils and snares and suffered death to share the Good News! I think of the beginning of Cullowhee Baptist Church, located now on the campus of Western Carolina University. In 1821, a small number of people traveled over the Balsam Mountains to begin a new work of sharing the Good News here in what is now Jackson County.

One cannot think of Cullowhee Baptist Church without thinking of missions, both here at home and around the world. The church minutes reflect many references of money being collected for both foreign and local missions. Even though the congregation was small in number and money was scarce, they had a heart for missions...sharing the Good News!

Excerpt from the original minutes:

1889

12 Jan 1889 A collection of $2.00 taken to pay our missionary.

6 Jul 1889 A collection of $2.30 taken up for foreign missions.

2 Feb 1889 An offering of $3.17 taken up for foreign missions.

1890

5 Oct 1890 A collection of $2.25 was taken up for conventional missions.

1892

25 Jun 1892 A collection of $2.32 was taken up for conventional missions.

22 Jul 1892 A collection of 92 cents was taken up for the orphanage.

The church participates in many missions. One of the top-priorities of home missions is ministering to the college students from places all over the U.S. and those from foreign countries. It is a privilege and a joy to provide them a church home while they are away from their home. It is where we rejoice in the Good News together! Young interns have added much to our work here in our office and in the Sunday School classrooms.

College Outreach—WCU Cooperative Student Fellowship (CSF)

Located across the street from the Hunter Library on the campus of Western Carolina University, Cullowhee Baptist Church both loves and welcomes students. We offer students opportunities to practice their faith within a multi-generational congregation. Many students sing in our choir, work with our children, and participate in worship. College events are led in part by CBC's Music Minister Steve Baxley. On March 27, 2011, Steve Baxley came before the Deacon Board to present the "Ministry Covenant of Cullowhee Baptist Church and the WCU Cooperative Student Fellowship." The following is an excerpt from that presentation:

The WCU Cooperative Student Fellowship (CSF) began as part of the student ministry of Cullowhee Baptist Church in 2009 and was officially recognized as a student organization in 2010 "for the purpose of growing students in their faith, love, and service to God and developing their understanding of God's mission in the world."

• Because of our shared vision we are committed to supporting each other as we minister to and provide ministry opportunities for college students.

• Cullowhee Baptist Church is happy to provide space for the Cooperative Student Fellowship to meet and hold its activities and to assist in providing financial support for CSF ministries.

• Cullowhee Baptist Church and the Cooperative Student Fellowship will promote student participation in each other's programs and activities and encourage involvement in opportunities for service and leadership.

• We will pray for each other's spiritual growth as individuals and as communities of faith as we discern God's direction for our lives.

Presenting the Cooperative Student Fellowship pledge to the congregration, CSF president Amanda Smith and Deacon Chairman Matthew Brown (Aug. 2011)

• We will seek ways to work together as we minister to the needs of students, the community, and the world around us.

• Members of the Cullowhee Baptist Church College Ministry Committee and the Cooperative Student Fellowship Leadership Team will hold an open meeting at least once each semester to facilitate cooperation between our ministries. During the school year, the Cooperative Student Fellowship college group meets at 7:00 pm every Monday in the fellowship hall at CBC.

Other local missions have included participating in the Christmas Store, conducting services at the nursing homes, Vacation Bible School, Jackson County Jail Ministry, White Christmas, and Feeding the Children Summer Program. Foreign missions have included CBF Global Missions, Lottie Moon, Shoe Box Christmas, supporting the missionaries in Helena, Arkansas; the Podgaiskys in the Ukraine; WNC Slavic Ministry in Asheville; the ministry in Haiti and Liberia, plus many, many more.

Excerpt from Dr. Jeffrey Vickery —

"Feeding the Children Summer Program"

From June 20 to August 5, 2011, we officially served 702 lunches at the two sites in Cullowhee. To successfully complete this summer's ministry, we started out in June with 148 volunteer times needed (that's the number of volunteer slots we had to fill). These were filled by 56 individual volunteers including help from three churches (Cullowhee Baptist, St. David's Episcopal, and the Summit), two businesses (SECU of Cullowhee, Dan Kidd's CPA office), and two organizations/groups (Cullowhee Daybreak Rotary, Cullowhee Valley School).

The food for the children was provided by MANNA Foodbank in Asheville, with organizational leadership from Jim Hill at Jackson County Public Schools. Their support and help with this ministry is necessary for us to feed even one child. They have been great partners in ministry, strong advocates for the children in this county, and willing hands and voices for meeting the food needs of all of us.

The first "Feeding the Children Summer Program" in June, 2010. Volunteer shown: Kathy Lovedahl

Mission teams have gone throughout the world to places like São Paulo, Brazil; Honduras; Helena, Arkansas; West Virginia; and New York to share the Good News with our fellow believers and others. We are confident and rejoice together in Jesus' promise "...and surely I am with you always, to the very end of the age!" His command to do missions truly gives purpose to life.

Following are some photos of church missions through the years

Vacation Bible School

First Established at Cullowhee Baptist Church in 1928

1970s

Bottom row: Laura Moore, Amy Miller, Matthew Martin; 2nd row: Samuel Barall, Tina Galloway, Tammy Pool, Laura Miller, Rebecca Moore, Eric Hinson; 3rd row: Roxanne Bryson, Amy Faircloth, Mitzi Searcy, Amanda Chancellor, Vic Bryson, Dianne Cook, Cordelia Chancellor, Lucille Painter; 4th row: Tom Lord, Youth Dir., Louella Brown, Cydney Hinson, Greg Galloway, Mrs. Barrett, Sara Jane Hinson, Carlula Bryson; 5th row: Rev. Jack Hinson, Lora Ponder, Ann Martin, Sherry Miller, Kay Cosper, Kathy Vosecky, Kathy Lovedahl

1990s

No names were listed on this photo.

2000s

Bottom row: Emily Melrose, ?, Brooke or Ashley Obragon, Adam Melrose, Deserrae Obragon, Michele Mauldin, Seth Kuhen, Greg Lockhart. Back row: Mark Melrose, Patrick Rice, Irene Hooper, Iva Jane Mull, Amy Ammons Garza

Glimpses of Youth Missions

Skyland Nursing Home, 2008

Painting UCM Ramp, 2008

Ham Donation, 2008

Trick or Treat for Canned Goods for UCM, 2009

Heifer International Children and Youth Misson 2008—Current

by Beth Baxley

In 2008, the children's Sunday School class felt led to support Heifer International as an ongoing mission project. We could have purchased a bee hive for a needy family for $30 or a heifer for $500 or a number of other farm animals at costs between those two. Our children, however, are so generous, and love to think big. They said, "Let's buy an ark!" An ark consists of 21 pairs or groups of animals, all useful to needy families around the world for earning a lifetime income. One of the hallmarks of Heifer is to "pass on the gift." This means that a villager who receives an ark animal promises to pass along some of its offspring to another person in the village. In this way, entire communities can create a sustaining income.

The children have done a number of fundraisers over the years, including making and selling snacks, organizing and serving a church covered-dish dinner, selling wooden Christmas ornaments representing the ark animals (made by Ron Yount), and selling hats and scarves hand-knit by our friend Evey Mumm in Florida. VBS (held at Cullowhee United Methodist Church and supported by several Jackson County churches), has donated nearly $500 over the past two summers.

Some of the children who began this endeavor: Tessa Davis, Ally Vickery, Brittney Collins, Alyssa Collins, Rebecca Fox, and Abigail Fox.

Ark animals made by Ron Yount

To date we have collected $3, 028.22 toward our $5,000 ark goal! The children would like to thank our church family and all the VBS contributors for the amazing outpouring of support. It is a wonderful work in progress and has utilized so much creativity, enthusiasm and compassion. To learn more, go to http://www.heifer.org.

Pastor's home for Jersualem Bautista Iglesia, Satellite City, Honduras, 1991

Check presented for orphanage in Morocco, 2003

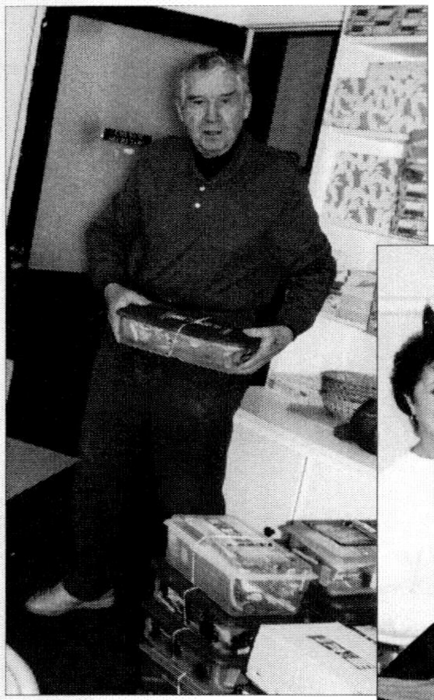

*Jerry Rice packing **Samaritan's Purse** Operation Shoe-boxes, 2000*

***Sunrise Service,** Chef Tammy Gaetano*

***Wednesday Night Meals:** Bonnie Hooper, Christine Crawford, Delores Nicholson, Ruby Coggins, Jean Painter; 1999*

***Relay for Life Cancer Fundraiser** 2001*

***Arkansas Mission Trip,** June 2005*

***Delta Jewels:** Mission for teenage girls in Helena, Ark. Created by Together for Hope; brought to Cullowhee by Reverend Wanda Kidd, 2010*

ЕСА
СМЕРТЬ, А ДАР
ИНСУСЕ.

Slavic Ministry in Asheville

Ramp Building

CBFNC Mission Work Days

Worship at Hermitage May 15, 2011

WMU—Woman's Missionary Union
First Mentioned in Cullowhee Baptist Church Minutes in 1926

The Principle of Purpose. Organization is always a means to an end and not an end in itself. The purpose of Woman's Missionary Union is to teach missions, lead persons to participate in missions, provide organization and leadership for special missions projects of the church, and provide and interpret information regarding the work of the church and denomination. Organization is the way people are related together to get these jobs done.

Excerpt from the original minutes:
1926
17 Jul 1926 First mention of WMU in minutes
1929
"A vote of thanks should be tendered to Bro. J.S. Trotter for carrying the Senior BYPU to East La Port and a vote of thanks be extended the Woman's Missionary Society for entertaining the BYPU."

The WMU organization consisted of Baptist Women, for women age 30 years and up; Baptist Young Woman for women 18 through 39 years old; Acteens for girls 12 through 17; Girls in Action (GA's) for girls six through 11; Mission Friends for boys and girls birth through five.

Cullowhee Baptist Church has WMU records from 1926 through 2000. At one time the group was called the "Dix Gap Circle of the WMU." The women of the church have done tremendous work for missions throughout all the years. Through the leadership of the WMU (greatly influenced by church member Annie Hoyle), the women of the church have been active in strengthening the church through prayer, education, contributions, and keeping before the church the purpose of missions. Annie Hoyle served in many capacities throughout the years of her membership, providing profound leadership.

The practice of giving to missions continues at Cullowhee Baptist Church today, led by the Missions Committee and co-pastors Dr. Jeffrey and Reverend Tonya Vickery.

Annie Hoyle

WMU Fellowship

Gladys Parker was for many years one of our oldest members; she was very active in Woman's Missionary Union, WMU they called it. The WMU spearheaded a lot of missions work that went on in the church: for example, fundraisers for the Broyhill Children's Home, home missions and foreign missions. But they also had a lot of fun. One time they had a fashion show. It was called a Tacky Show, and they all dressed up in clothes they had probably had 50 years. They wore big flowers in their hair. Once, one of the ladies, Martha Lou Stillwell, who was about 4'10" and about as big as your little finger, was going to Hawaii. We recently found a picture of that WMU group all dressed up in leis, and they looked like they had either been to or were coming from Hawaii. They had a big party for Martha Lou.

1960, Hawaiian party: (bottom)Kathy Vosecky, Martha Lou Stillwell, Bessie Moses, Ethel Hooper, Gladys Parker, Louella Brown; (middle) Thelma Harrill, Betty Jean Ash Brook; (top) Irene Crawford, Maude Sherrill, Mrs. Ashbrook, Pearl Mashburn, Frances Coggins, Winnie Killian, Mildred Norton, Phoebe Hooper, Lucille Painter

---

Stained-Glass Doors to the Baptistry

The stained-glass doors currently in the baptistry were installed in June 1993. Jack Barnett worked more than three months to create and install the beautiful doors. A member of the Cullowhee Baptist Church from 1953, Barnett served the church as a choir member, choir director, church clerk, committee member, and chairman of numerous committees. His donation of the stained-glass work measured 79 inches by 89 inches and contained two permanent panels and two moveable sections. Using traditional Christian symbols, the work is a lush arrangement of color and design and contains glass matching some of the church's existing stained glass. The colors in the panels are as symbolic as the designs. The blue represents the Father, yellow the Son, and red the Holy Ghost.

Baptist Student Union (BSU) Activities

Beginning in 1942, the church worked closely with the state convention's Baptist Student Union, an organization to help Baptist students in college settings. Then the church offered the BSU use of a "prayer shack" on church property. The first full-time BSU director, Colin Godwin, came about 1960. He used the church to conduct his programs. In 1965, a BSU building was constructed (with Jim Searcy as brick mason).

Some Past Campus Ministers:
Reverend Joe Clontz
Reverend Joe David Fore
Reverend Winston Hardman
Reverend Wanda Kidd

BSU students in 1970s

Reverend Wanda Kidd with husband Dan Kidd and son Stanton, 1999

Interfaith Christian Dramas—*The Trail of Light* and *Mary Did You Know*

Produced at Cullowhee Baptist Church 1999—2008

The Trail of Light

This original interfaith Christian drama had a long run at Cullowhee Baptist Church. The drama told the story of the lineage of Christ, one generation after another, from Adam and Eve on down to and beyond the birth of Christ—many stories of the Bible came alive to re-create the most wondrous Christmas story ever told. Having the play at Cullowhee Baptist Church was appropriate, for the congregation represented the first church formed in the history of the area (west of the Balsams).

The drama had its beginnings during Christmas of 1998 when 40 men and women at Cullowhee Baptist Church came forward with candles as names were called for some of the ancestors of Jesus. Etheree Chancellor, secretary of the church, started thinking about staging this drama the following year on the church steps. In 1999, Chancellor asked Amy Ammons Garza, an author who was a member of the church, to write the play. Garza agreed. Many meetings were called in which the two women discussed the project with Cullowhee Baptist's Pastor Mike Vanzura and Gene McAbee, a member of the Cullowhee Methodist Church, and others from both churches. The script grew as the discussions went more into depth, until it was no longer a minor skit, but a major drama. With the idea that each person in the lineage of Christ should carry a lighted torch, the play was named *The Trail of Light*; the torches represented the long line of generations it took to arrive at the birth of Jesus. A millennium section was written by Gene McAbee to close the drama, and reach out to the future.

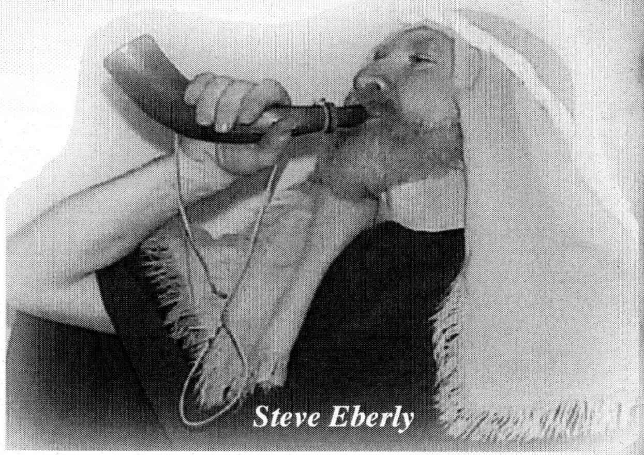

Steve Eberly

In the fall of 1999, with a script in hand, the two women asked Barbara Eberly from Saint Mary's Catholic Church of Sylva to help with costumes, and they found a young student from Western Carolina University, Jeff Hedgecock, to be the director. Then they began asking people from other churches to be a part of the production.

Barbara Eberly

By the time the play was produced, it had expanded to also include the following churches: Calvary Baptist of Sylva, Christ the King Catholic Student Center, Cullowhee Presbyterian, East Sylva Baptist, Lifeway Christian, Sylva Church of God, and the Tuckaseigee Baptist Church.

Soon, over 100 people from these churches and people who did not attend any church on a regular basis, came together to tell the great story for *The Trail of Light*.

Catch the Spirit of Appalachia, a local nonprofit that had produced a Christmas drama earlier, donated all their costumes to the production. Local ladies began sewing; fabric stores began donating material and jewelry for crowns; colleges donated the use of lights; church members donated the time to assemble the torches (thread cones donated from a carpet plant from Georgia with flashlights inside, covered with material); the county parks department brought outside seating; and Doreyl Ammons Cain, artist, drew the logo for the production. Writers and graphic artists donated their services for marketing and design; and as the drama came down to rehearsals, nine local musicians volunteered their entertaining talents for the scheduled two performances.

Planned as an outdoor drama that first year, the rehearsals brought so many men, women, children, and live animals that it looked as if people from the old world were actually roaming around the grounds of the church. It was a wondrous thing seeing the dramatization of the lineage of Christ come alive with beautiful song, music, costumes, and heartfelt acting. On the night of the first production, the narrator, Reverend Jack Hinson, Hospital Chaplain for Harris Regional Hospital, was heard to tell the actors, "Before you step one foot out in the first scene, know that this production is already a success...because actors of many faiths are all working together!"

The year 2000 brought so many more people to help with the production that now the drama had members from 27 congregations. Barbara Eberly took over the director's job, and Suzanne Kehrberg, an outstanding local choreographer, came on board, along with Pastor Roy Burnett (also a radio announcer)

taking on the job of sound and audio for the drama that had now been moved inside the church because of the weather. With the increase of the number of people and props, Dianne Yount accepted the job of stage manager and recruited a stage crew.

To increase marketing endeavors, the drama created a float for the Christmas Parade held annually in the county seat of Sylva, on which many members of the cast represented the play. In addition, a talented 13-year-old Josh Bulla (who played a lyre as young David), and his grandmother, Ruby (playing Naomi), visited other local churches to acquaint the congregations with the scope of the drama. Also in 2000, on the nights of the performances, luminaries were added on the sidewalks at the church and along the street for blocks on each side, lighting the trail to *The Trail of Light.*

In 2001 the drama team increased to include Ray Menze and Amy Garza as assistant directors. Chancellor and Garza entered the Western North Carolina Community Booth contest at the Mountain State Fair in Fletcher and won first place. The $250 prize helped to produce better brochures, and information posters, and update the banners.

In this third year of operation, the cast and crew increased to 150 people from 29 churches in five surrounding counties. A musical pre-show was added, with the talents of the Cullowhee United Methodist Church Handbell Choir, local singers, Celtic dancers, and musicians. The behind-the-scenes crews grew tremendously to help handle the many different scenes.

For 2002, the cast was so large that practices were handled by four directors, each group practicing at different times. Producers, directors, stage and sound crew, narrator, actors, actresses, artists, seamstresses, dancers, musicians, children, animals, entire families—all involved in this production were local community members, all volunteering their time to be a part of this experience.

Once again, *The Trail of Light* won first place in the North Carolina Mountain State Fair. This year, the drama team came up with the idea to create coloring books using the script of the play, inserting scripture references for each scene so children could follow the "Trail of Light" through the Bible. An Atlanta-based family of artists—Elizabeth, Jesse, and Rachel Evans—donated their artistic talents to illustrate the coloring book. This concept and the amount of community support helped to once again win first place at the fair. The coloring books were sold for ($5) to help defray printing costs of the coloring books and expense of the production, since no admission was charged. Also in 2002, The Trail of Light drama team and the new pastors of Cullowhee Baptist Church, the Reverends Jeffrey and Tonya Vickery, organized their first fundraising brunch, donating time, food, and decorations to help with the growing costs of production. Chancellor and Garza joined others in a trip to Pennsylvania to view methods of production in the Christian drama *Daniel in the Lion's Den.* While on that trip, they found oil lamps appropriate for the kings in *The Trail of Light.*

Many other dreams necessary for the growth of the drama came true in 2002. An interested benefactor donated special lighting for the church, WestCare at Harris Regional Hospital donated the funds to purchase two spotlight systems, Gail and Joe Nolen of Whittier donated expert time and funds for newly designed torches held by all actors in the lineage of Christ, local ladies produced many new costumes, and the church improved the sound system.

In 2003 the drama team sponsored another brunch, raising an additional $500. Some additional costumes were made by local people, and our directors now included Penny Graham, a wonderful actress and children's director. We had cast members from over 34 churches! The continuing growth of *The Trail of Light* testified to the successful blending of faiths working together for a common good.

In June of 2004, Smyth & Helwys Publishers became interested in the drama, and *The Trail of Light* was published as an "E-Drama" on their website. Also, the Great Smoky Mountains Railroad offered a deal for *The Trail of Light* cast members. In groups of four in costume, the cast was given a free train ride to lead the singing on the train during *The Polar Express* excursion.

During 2004, TOL also provided a Gingerbread Mountain Church contest, led by Judy Teague, a cast member. Hot chocolate was also provided out on the lawn after the performances, hosted by Mary Jo and Wayne Cobb, members of Tuckasegee Baptist Church. A new director, Katie Hoyle, was added.

At the meeting to review the play, the team discussed the time it took to procure 150 people each year. The consensus from the drama team was the number needed to be reduced, so Amy Ammons Garza and Barbara Eberly began to think about producing another play that would follow in path of *The Trail of Light.*

2005—*Mary Did You Know*

In its eighth year of production, the Trail of Light Interfaith Drama Team brought to the public on the second weekend of December at Cullowhee Baptist Church, a new play entitled *Mary Did You Know*. With a 50-member cast and crew derived from regional congregations, the story of Jesus from birth until maturity brought, as some members of the audience said, "a time of peace and refection as to what the Christmas season is all about." The music of the production included such solos as "Ava Maria," "Magnificat," "Oh Holy Night," "Mary Did You Know," "Love is the Greatest Gift of All," and "When God Dips His Pen of Love in My Heart." These selections were sung by Henry Wong, Mary-Kira Wilson, Karen Lindsay, Katherine Collins, Erin Nicholson, Sarajane Hinson Melton, and Paula Fox. The Angel Chorus and Children's Angel Chorus shared "Angels We Have Heard On High," "Away in a Manger," "Tell Me the Story of Jesus," and "God Is So Good."

During the performance, Mary Ferrick, percussionist, linked the nine scenes together with Middle Eastern drums and cymbals, while the voice of Chaplain Jack Hinson added just the right touch as the narrator. Written to show portions of the birth and life of Jesus, the drama gave glimpses of Jesus as a baby, at two years old, at twelve years old and at maturity. The story line switched back and forth between scenes in Bethlehem and at King Herod's court. Under the direction of Maribeth Ayers and musical direction of Pam Dengler, the interfaith cast and crew demonstrated the dedication of their faith by bringing this first performances of a new play to a rousing success! The community supported the play by filling the auditorium for both performances.

Regional congregations involved in this new play were Sylva First Baptist, Sylva First Methodist, Sylva Presbyterian, Sylva St. Mary's Catholic, Scotts Creek Baptist, East Sylva Baptist,

Lovedale Baptist, Love's Chapel Methodist, Bryson City Mt. Zion Missionary Baptist, Waynesville Seventh-Day Adventist, Cullowhee St. David's Episcopal, Cullowhee Methodist, and Cullowhee Baptist.

From 2005 through 2008, The Trail of Light drama team produced *Mary Did You Know* with this smaller cast and a new director, Teresa Eberly, with zeal and much success, bringing many visitors to the church. Teresa had a lovely voice, and added the song "Lord of the Dance" to the end of the show.

The last couple of years, a different ending brought another songstress into the play. Victoria Cassey McDonald, costumed in slave attire, gave a touching performance with the song "Sweet Little Jesus Boy."

One of the best results of the productions *The Trail of Light* and *Mary Did You Know* was the involvement of the youth of the church. Many of them advanced from playing a non-speaking part, such as a shepherd, to a speaking part or a dancing part, learning all the while the stories of the Bible, and gaining self-confidence as they looked forward to an exciting event year after year.

After the 2008 production was completed, Etheree Chanellor and Amy Ammons Garza, with heartfelt thanks to all those who had spent years participating in both production ministries with them, deemed it was time to retire the plays.

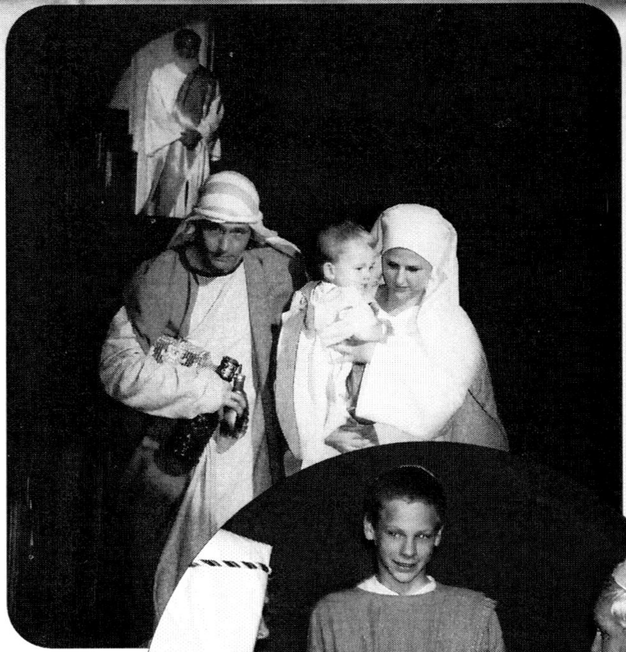

Peace be with you!
(Luke 24:36)

Glimpses of *The Trail of Light* and *Mary Did You Know*

Glimpses of *The Trail of Light* and *Mary Did You Know*

Some History of Our Fellowship

by Etheree Chancellor

Church Camping Trips

The first Cullowhee Baptist Church camping trip took place in the fall of 1985 at Smokemont Campground in the Smokies with Rev. Jack Hinson and Steve Baxley as organizers. Rev. Jack Hinson had his wife Sara and son, Eric with us. Eric had a grand new pair of tennis shoes. Eric and my youngest daughter Amanda were about the same age. Lauren Baxley, daughter of Beth and Steve, and younger than Eric went wading in the cold, rocky stream. After the wade Eric took off his new tennis shoes and put them beside the fire and the first thing we knew, they were completely melting. Others on this camping trip were my husband Paul, Myra and Micky Clements, and one set of their parents.

Black Rock Mountain, Georgia, was the chosen spot for the Cullowhee Baptist Campers in August of 1990. It was very secluded and private. There were lean-tos but not enough for everyone. Some of us set our tents up in the lean-tos; others just camped out as usual in the open woods. There was an old log house there which we were not allowed to go into, and it probably would have been dangerous if we had. It was so old, the logs were chinched with mud. We did eat under the porch roof, which had a dirt flooring. We got water from a very good stream that was piped directly from within the earth. After dinner we had a sing-a-long with Jeff Davis playing his guitar. John Denver's songs were the most popular ones on this trip. Those present were Steve, Beth, and Lauren Baxley; Barb and Jeccica Barlow; Jeff and Sandy Davis; Paul, Melanie, Zach and Matt White; Bryan Hunter; Amanda; and myself.

Amanda and Etheree Chancllor
Black Rock Mountain, Georgia

Sandy Davis, Jessica Barlow, Lauren Baxley, Beth Baxley, and Barb Barlow at Black Rock Mountain, Georgia

We were in Cataloochee camping at the group campsite when Bill Mincey, who moved to heaven several years ago, played the guitar and the banjo. Bill had been playing the guitar for a little while and we'd been singing along. He laid down the guitar and picked up the banjo. Well, after he had been pickin' the banjo for a few minutes a deer came out of the woods and walked up within two feet of the banjo and just looked at it as Bill continued to play. The rest of us just froze. Finally the deer turned and walked away. Bill, Paul, Matt, and Zach enjoyed fishing in the Pigeon River. The river was a fun place to wade and play for all. Others camping were Margie Atkinson; Steve and Beth Baxley; Bonnie, Jeremy, and Wesley Mincey; Galen Ernest; Jeff and Sandy Davis; Barbara and Jessica Barlow; Polly and Clifton McGinnis; Bobby Joe Conley; and Paul and I. Our son Charles and his friend Lena came to enjoy one of our meals.

Another camping trip was at Cade's Cove. I had a couple of college girls, Sarah Frady of Little Canada and the other whose name I don't remember, with me and my youngest daughter, Amanda. We got there early to put up the tent first and claim the campsite. There was a bear behind a tree, and one of the girls grabbed her camera and ran out to the road to take a picture. Well, when she did, the bear came down on all fours, staring at us. Of course we all started backing up and the bear turned away.

This trip was the biggest group of all times: Bob and Janice Holt; Jack and Pam Galloway; Bonnie and Bill Mincey with son Jeremy; Steve and Beth Baxley and daughter Lauren; Vista Boggs; Paul, Melanie, Matt, and Zach White; and Debra and Leon Martin and son Nick. After dinner, we were sitting around the camp fire enjoying the warmth when a beautiful raccoon sneaked up to the table where someone had left soda cans. The raccoon stared at us as he slowly slipped one of his front paws into one of the cans, backed up a little, turned and ran. He continued this until he had gotten all the cans from the table. The skunks made their rounds in and around and under our chairs eating dropped food. The kids were warned to be quiet and they did a great job.

Later in the night, we could hear a bear slamming the doors to the trash cans, coming closer and closer toward our campsite. The whole Cove was filled with campers, and so I unzipped the tent and looked out. I could make out the form of the bear. Three of us campers had fairly new minivans, but the Holts had the red minivan. The bear climbed up on one of the vans. We couldn't see whose it was, and about that time Bill Mincey came out with a flashlight yelling "Get outta here! Get outta here!"

Beth Baxley asked Steve, "Steve, what's going on?"

"There's a bear in the campground," Steve answered.

"Ok," she said, 'let's just go back to sleep. Bill will take care of it."

We all knew when Bill was around he would take care of any problems, and if he needed help, the Whites were right there ready and waiting. I yelled to Bill and asked him if he wanted me to go get the park ranger. He said yes, so I went to get the park ranger. Since I did not wear my glasses, I could not see well, but I felt around enough on the phone till I found the 0 for the operator. She kept telling me I had to deposit money.

And I kept telling her I didn't have any money, and that I couldn't see money if I had it. I explained to her what was going on, and finally she put me through to the police department in Sevierville, TN. "Well, we'll take care of it; we'll find you a park ranger," said the policewoman. The park ranger had told me if we had trouble to come knock on this particular door of the ranger station. I did, but he didn't answer. Nobody answered. But by the time I got back to the camp site, the bear had gone and had also tried to get into a truck with a camper on the back to get to food. The next morning we found these beautiful bear marks on the Holt's new red van where the bear had slid down the front window and on down the hood. It seemed a long time before the ranger came.

Another time Jack Hinson; the Henry's, the Minceys, who by this time had a couple of boys; Barbara and Jessica Barlow; Steve and Beth Baxley; Micky and Myra Clements; and I were camping at Tremont in the Smokies. Keith and Donna brought a huge borrowed tent that six or so people could sleep in. Just as everyone was settling in for the evening, it began to rain. The more it rained the worse the tent leaked on one end. I had a large van, so Barbara, Jessica, and I got in the back door of the van, putting our feet under the seat and our head at the back doors in hopes of getting some sleep while others fought the rain. As we settled in the van, Jessica who was just old enough to talk well, asked, "Mom, are we camping yet?" Barbara and I cracked up.

These are a few of outstanding stories, of good times and experiences we had.

XYZ Senior Adult Group

Rev. Joe Yelton organized a senior adult group that was named XYZ – EXtra Years of Zest. I usually drove the seniors to wherever we went when Joe wasn't available. Pelham Thomas assisted from time to time. Mildred Norton, who was a fun event coordinator, planned many wonderful trips and parties for the XYZers. She enjoyed decorating her home and getting the Dills Sisters to perform for us with their fiddles, at her Christmas parties. Shopping trips to Knoxville; trips on the Parkway and lunch at Pisgah Inn; Amacalola Falls, GA; Dillard House, GA; Silver Springs, FL; The Barter Theatre in Abington, VA; and Mars Hill, NC, were only a few of our memorable trips.

Joe planned a cruise for the group, a new kind of experience for most. The

Mildred & Ben Norton, Pearl Mashburn, Ruby Cagle, Moquita Crawford, Joe Yelton, Percy & Gladys Parker, Howard & Lois McNeil, Cathie Clayton

XYZ members were Carlula Bryson; Ollie Burkett; Cathie Clayton; Moqueta Crawford; Fred and Veree Dills; and later Fred and Thelma Dills after Veree moved to heaven; Sue and Harry Duke; Irene and Elmer Hooper; Pearl Mashburn; Jane and Stedman Mitchell; Mildred and Ben Norton; Lucille Painter; Gladys Parker; Jane Roberts; Wilma Smith; Pelham and Marie Thomas; and Cathy and Eugene Vosecky. Others who retired and joined in later years were Paul Chancellor; Ruby Coggins; Charles and Pam Hill; Bonnie Hooper; Delores Nicholson; Jean Painter; Harriet Parker; Shirley Smith; JoAnne Sutton; Dianne Yount; and Delaine Wilkes. Friends from neighboring churches also joined in the fun trips: Juanita Burrell, Doris Clemmons, Lucy Crawford, Libby Etherton, Rose Hooper, Stella Parker, Hilda Pasour, and Jerdie Stevens.

Oh, we always had fun with XYZers... they were just a hoot. When we went to Pennsylvania, we went to a train museum in Amish Country. We take side roads and rode around, occasionally stopping to buy pies, which we'd share in the motel at night. It was just a good time with the XYZers because they were always up for a trip.

Next to the last trip I planned, my husband Paul drove. We first visited First Baptist Church of Charleston and were amazed at the graves all the way up to the church building. We spent one night on Tybee Island and ate at this dumpy restaurant where the food was good. We toured the lighthouse there as well as the brick walk along the water in Savannah. Cathie Clayton was 80 and the oldest person with us. She climbed all three of the lighthouses that we visited. She was amazing. I didn't climb any because I have a fear of heights.

I remember one time when we went to the Dillard House to eat on our way to Amicalola Falls in Georgia. I had never seen this done before and I thought it was so

XYZ South of the Boarder party: top: Fred Dills & Cathie Clayton; bottom: Pelham & Marie Thomas

funny: every one of those women had plastic bags in their purses. The waitresses brought out all this food for us at the Dillard House, and when we were all finished eating, the ladies took those plastic bags and filled them with leftovers. Later, I realized every time we went on a trip they did this. When we got to Amicalola Falls, this prized food is what we had for lunch. To see the tall waterfalls and walk down all those woodens steps was breathtaking in more ways than one.

Charles and Pam Hill planned a wonderful trip to Hot Springs and other places in Georgia, including attending President Jimmy Carter's Sunday School Class in Plains. What a treat! The Hills and the Younts continue to treat us with day trips and picnics as does Rev. Dr. Jeffrey Vickery, our present pastor.

As health problems developed, fewer people were able to prepare the Wednesday morning breakfasts at the church and the trips dwindled. A few luncheon trips are still taken occasionally.

Glimpses of Church Fellowship

1980s--Seated: D. Granthan, M. Millwood, D. Bryant, L. Ponder, R. Gobel, S. Wood, E. Chancellor. Standing: S. McDowell, P. Vickes, M. Searcy, J. Galloway, P. Galloway, L. Granthan, P. Thomas, J. Edwards, J. Gobel, J. Bryant, B. Ward, P. Chancellor

1970--Costume Party
Beth and Steve Baxley

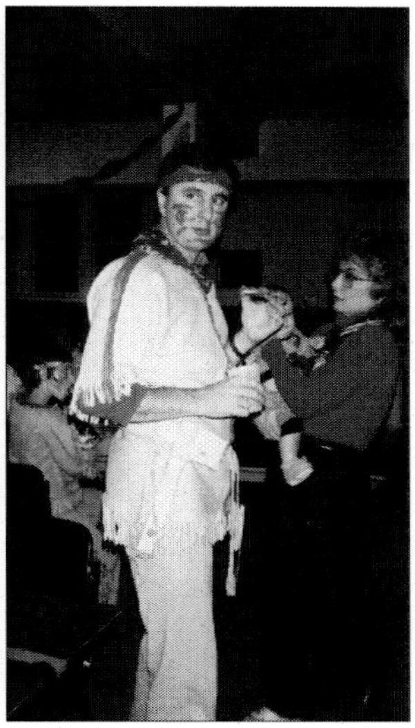

1991--Costume Party
Jeff Davis and Beth Baxley

1973 Homecoming Celebration--
(standing) Percy Parker, Lillian Hirt, Joe David Fore.
(seated) Pearl Mashburn, Lucille Painter, Lorraine Norton, Winnie Killian, Sara Sue Duke, Gladys Parker

XYZ Club trip through Pisgah Forest and local Areas: June, 1990.
Etheree Chancellor, Lois and Howard McNeil,
Ollie Burkett, Mary Helderman, and Mrs. Coggins.

Glimpses of Church Fellowship

Valentine's Day
King, Queen, & Prince 2008

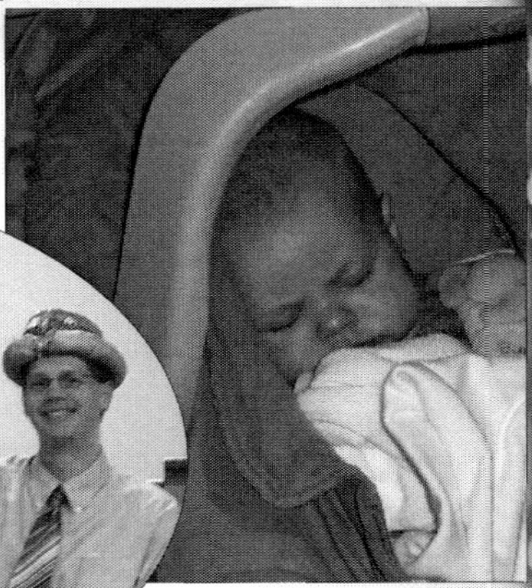

Souper Bowl Sunday 2009

Steve Baxley's Surprise
Anniversary Party--500th Sunday as
Choir Director • March 1, 2009

Glimpses of Church-Community Fellowship

XYZers Presidential Tour, Carter Trip—October 25-27, 2002
President Jimmy Carter, 2002 Nobel Peace Prize Winner, Etheree Chancellor; Pam Hill; Deloris Nicholson; Jane Mitchell; Stedman Mitchell (behind Jane); Charles Hill (behind Stedman); Jayne Roberts; Juanita Burrell (First Baptist, Sylva); Elmer Hooper; Marie Leatherwood (First Baptist, Sylva); Irene Hooper; Doris Clemmons (First Baptist, Sylva); Stella Parker (Tuckaseigee Baptist); Dianne Yount; and Rosalyn Carter.
Photo made beside Maranatha Baptist Church, Plains, Georgia.

XYZers Tybee Island & Charleston, SC—May 2003 Trip
Paul Chancellor (driver), Etheree Chancellor, Cordelia Chancellor Meyer, Shelby Ray Meyer, Bonnie Hooper, Libby Etherton, Cathie Clayton, Jackie Angel, Shirley Smith, Doris Clemmons, Stella Parker, Jean Painter, Jayne Roberts, Hilda Pasour

Glimpses of Church Building Improvement Fundraising

Lora (Pokey) Watson--Fall Color Festival, October 1999

Pat Angel, Ed Robison, Peggy Angel, Carroll & Mary Jo Jones, Brenda Watson Gray—yard sale 2002

Sue Duke & Harriet Parker making jelly for yard sale, 1999

Harriet Mashburn Parker & Billie Crawford Jones, yard sale, 2003

Bonnie Hooper & Allison Melrose

Emily & Allison Melrose

Fashion Show Luncheon 2000

Harriet Mashburn Parker & Gladys Parker, quilting, 2000

Youth Clogging Team

by Etheree Chancellor

Amanda Chancellor, Elizabeth Patterson, Vista Boggs, Amy Buchanan

Several Cullowhee Baptist youth were on the Cullowhee Clogging team. Not only did they dance at the 1986 World's Fair in Canada, they performed on the big board-walk at Ocean City, MD, during one of their mission trips. Some of the kids dressed up as clowns and invited people to come in to the mission church to have hot dogs. Eric and David Lovedahl, who dressed up as clowns, were really quiet in church and didn't say a whole lot. But when they got on those clown suits and were out on the beach, their personality just bloomed. They were a hoot!

Amy Buchanan, Corinne Yelton, Vista Boggs, Elizabeth Patterson

One place we went, a campground, the owner had been telling the mission-ary, "No, you can't come in. I'm not a Christian and I don't want anything to do with that." After we called the mis-sionary and asked her if we could use the cloggers up there, she went to the owner and said, "I have something free to give you if you will let us have Bible study in your camp-ground."

The stage was like one found in a gold mining town, in a saloon. He thought about it a few days and decided. The lady missionary was told, "Okay, you can you do that. If you let your people come here and dance free, then you can have Bible stud-ies in my camp-ground."

We did, and as a result the owner of the campground became a Christian. The youth held Bible studies at As-sateague State Park with the wild horses roaming around. That's one thing about the youth that really stands out in my mind.

(The cloggers were led by Bonnie Mincey.)

Glimpses of Youth Activities

By Etheree Chancellor

Another thing that really sticks out in my mind is the kids in the youth group when Wanda Kidd was youth minister. Many days Wanda was down at the school to greet the youth and talk with them after their day of school.

Some of the youth at that time were: Roxanne and Vic Bryson, Amy Buchanan, Amanda Chancellor, Lora Cox, Greg Galloway, Louie Lusk, Eric and David Lovedahl, Kerry Hall, Amy Millwood, Elizabeth Patterson, Karen and Kevin Rice, Edward Wike, Shannon and Sherrie Wike, and Shannon Wilkes. Usual chaperons for trips included: The Revs. Wanda Kidd and Joe Yelon, Corinne Yelton, Mary Helderman, Bill and Bonnie Mincey, and Etheree Chancellor. Jake and Rosemary yelton would sometimes go on the trips with their parents.

Pioneer Plunge Youth Retreat
Todd Murdock, Susan Morris, Therese Murdock

Youth Trip with Ron & Dianne Yount

Bowling Trip
Wanda & Bethany Kidd

Bethany Kidd

Lauren Baxley

Vacation Bible School Picnic, July, 1989

Youth Outings and Activities
2007–2011

Glimpses of a Sunday at Cullowhee Baptist Church, 2011

Glimpses of a Sunday at Cullowhee Baptist Church, 2011

A visit to the cemetery

Some Memories From Members

Aunt Evie

by Mutt Morris

(Written May 7, 1995)

On April 18, I celebrated my birthday and Paul Revere's Ride. Right now I am not sure which came first. But I was not the only one in Cullowhee having a birthday. On April 18, 1895, Eva Lee Phillips was born. The daughter of Daniel and Isabella Phillips of Cullowhee, she was one of 13 children. Members of the Phillips family have been workers in and supporters of Cullowhee Baptist Church for many, many years. I grew up in Cullowhee and attended church with many of her nieces and nephews and always knew her as "Aunt Evie."

Aunt Evie remembers more than most people will ever know. She recalls her mother talking about the old log church, which she says was located in a clearing above the home of Bonnie and Austin Hooper. Even after the church was gone, for many years there was an area there that the Cullowhee Baptists used as a picnic ground on the site of the old church near the reservoir.

According to Aunt Evie, around 1918 plans were made to build a new church to be located nearer the school. This site was close to the location of our present church. She noted that it was known as the "white church." Before then the blacks and whites in the community had attended the same church. It took several years to complete the building. Much of the labor was furnished by the men after their regular working hours. Aunt Evie remembers with pleasure the oyster stew suppers where the members brought the food and then paid for the supper to raise money for construction materials. She remembers when it was replaced in 1929 by the current building.

Aunt Evie and Mildred Norton's mother were cousins and also good friends. They were baptized at the same time in the Tuckaseigee River just below the Cullowhee bridge across from Aunt Lil Grindstaff's house, which now has been completely restored and turned into apartments by Jim Moss.

Young Eva Phillips was educated at Edgar Stillwell's school, located where the steam plant now stands. The students brought their lunches in pails and sat out under the trees to eat. Three of the teachers whom she remembers well were Frank Brown, Sr., Prof. R.L. Madison and Edgar Stillwell.

Born and reared on Cane Creek in Jackson County, Eva continued to live there after her marriage to Oscar Ensley in 1921. They had three children: Charles, Ruth (a member of our church), and Doris. Oscar and Eva maintained a Christian home in rearing their family.

After Oscar passed away in 1980, Aunt Evie moved in with her daughter and son-in-law, Ruth and Clifford

Bryson. Doris Taylor has a home just behind Ruth's house, and Charles lives in Washington state. They have given her five grandchildren and "lots" of great-grandchildren. By her family she is described as the force that keeps her children, grandchildren, great-grandchildren, nieces, and nephews together generation after generation.

She says she thinks the Lord has left her here for a hundred years so she can take care of her family. She still fixes her own breakfast (biscuits and gravy) each morning and enjoys doing needle-work. Incidentally, don't call her or go to visit weekday afternoons—she's too busy watching her favorite "stories" on television.

It's a pleasure to honor Eva Lee Phillips Ensley as the oldest member of our church. In her life and her love of home and church, she serves as an inspiration to all of us.

Stories from Ruth Bryson & Linda Hughes

By Amy Ammons Garza
(October 1, 2011)

In talking with Ruth Bryson and Linda Hughes, we learn a little more about the lifestyle of the members of our church in the "old days."

Ruth, the daughter of "Aunt Evie," says she doesn't remember going to the old frame church, except for one time...it was to her little brother's funeral. She has attended Cullowhee Baptist Church her entire life. "Going to church was just something you did every Sunday," she says. "It didn't matter who the minister was, you just went! And in the beginning we walked every time. Cullowhee Baptist Church is MY church."

Ruth's cousin, Linda Hughes, told about how the church's Sunday School would give away paper bags of oranges, candy and nuts at Christmastime. "I so looked forward to it each year...it's something I'll never forget."

Another incident Linda mentioned had to do with another member of the church, Manley Brown. "As a teenager, I was working for Sunset Farms and not liking it very much. One day Manley and I were sitting at Cullowhee Cafe, and since we were both unhappy with our work, decided to go to High Hampton and apply for a job. When we got there, we were told we would be interviewed by a "Florida" lady. It scared us to death! We just knew she'd not hire us. Out comes this pretty blond-headed lady.

When I told her my name, she said, 'Are you Glenn Hughes' daughter?' Surprised, I said yes. Then she said 'I've spent many a night on the porch of your Uncle Rufe's house, at his all-night gospel singings in

Here Ruth Bryson shares her knowledge of tatting at the Patchwork Fabric Festival, 2011

Cullowhee. When do you want to come to work!' Wow...were we happy! Who'd ever think we'd get a job because of an all night singing!"

The house shown below is where the "singings" happened. In 1920, Rufus D. Phillips was the choir director for Cullowhee Baptist Church.

Daniel and Ruthie Farris Phillips Family (circa 1913)

At one time, all were members of Cullowhee Baptist Church:

Estella "Stel" Phillips Stephens
Frank Crawford
Effie "Eff" Crawford Hooper
Rufus Daniel "Rufe" Phillips
Eva "Evie" Phillips Ensley ***(Mother of Ruth Bryson)***
Nannie Phillips Coward
Verdie Marie Coward Miller (child)
Clara Bertha "Bertie" Smith Phillips
John Galliad Phillips
Jacob Daniel "Jake" Philips (child)
Fannie Blanche Phillips Painter
Robert Smith Phillips (child)
John Lee Crawford (standing)
Rebecca Emeline "Tid" Phillips Crawford (standing)
Willa Mae Crawford (child)
Betty Jane Phillips Hughes (seated)
Daniel Harrison "Dan" Phillips (seated)
Susanna Henson "Aunt Suckey" (seated)
Isabella Elizabeth "Ibby" Crawford Phillips (seated)
Bascombe Henry Hughes, Jr. (child on ground)
Glenn Lee Hughes (child on ground) ***(Father of Linda Hughes)***
Gertrude "Gertie" Crawford Kinsland (child on ground)
Wiley Crawford (child on ground)
Beulah Ethel Crawford Stephens (child on ground)

Prayer for Mother

By Irene Marriah Bishop Hooper

(Story passed down to me by my mother, Mattie Mae and my grandmother, Sally Bishop. Over the years, I've heard others repeat the same story.)

Mother had given birth over the years to seven babies, and now she was expecting number eight. All deliveries had taken place in our home with the assistance of Grandma Sally, who was a midwife.

Someone would go for the country doctor, but usually the babies came before he could get there. The two and one half miles of unpaved road up the Long Branch Road in Cullowhee to our big log house was slow traveling. When the doctor arrived, he would check the mother and baby over, record their names and then be on his way.

The number eight delivery didn't go well! Baby Jane had difficulty breathing, but she survived and was known as a blue baby. Mother was so weak, she fell into a coma and remained in this state for about ten days. The doctor told my daddy Grover and Grandma Sally there was nothing more he could do. He said, "Keep the noise down, keep the blinds closed, and let her sleep. She might come out of it in a few days."

Word quickly spread throughout the community. Neighbors offered to help, but there was little anyone could do.

During the ten days she was sleeping, Grandma would try to give her a sip of water, fruit juice, or warm soup every so often. In the meantime, the women of Cullowhee Baptist Church formed a prayer chain. Constant prayers were being offered up for Mother to be restored to health. In addition to taking turns, each morning three or four women walked up the long road to our house. They stood outside on the porch and prayed. Their prayers went like this: "Dear Lord, hear our prayers. Heal Mattie Mae. Her children and husband need her. If it be Your will, raise her up! Amen."

Irene & Elmer Hooper, 1990

On the tenth morning, Mother was aroused by a sound! Her first words were, "What's that noise I hear?" Grandma was so excited as she explained to her, "Your friends, the women from Cullowhee Baptist Church are praying for you. They have come each morning to pray while you were sleeping."

Mother's response was, "Oh! Please invite them in! Don't they know my house is a house of prayer?"

Needless to say, many prayers thanking God for His great mercy were uttered as they made their way to her bedside.

Mother slowly gained her strength back and baby Jane's condition improved. As a child I often heard my mother pray, "Lord, just let me live to see my children grow up."

Her prayers were aswered. After my daddy was killed in a traffic accident, Mother chose me out of the eight children to make her home with. What a blessing she was to our family for 29 years! My husband, Elmer, treated her with such great respect and our two children, Carl and Sandra, just idolized their *"Ma!"*

Sister Jane Bishop Gerner and Irene, 1999

Left: Irene's mother, Mattie Mae Morgan Bishop
Right: Irene's grandmother, Sally Phillips Bishop

Mother was almost 87 years old when the Lord called her to her eternal home.

She always spoke fondly of the women of Cullowhee Baptist Church and attributed her long life to their faithfulness in prayer and to the mercy of her Almighty and Powerful God!

Fond Memories of Cullowhee Baptist Church

by Kathy Lovedahl

Pete and Kathy Lovedahl, 1988

I have such fond memories of my 30-plus years at Cullowhee Baptist Church (CBC). I joined CBC in May or June of 1981. Pete and I married in the church sanctuary on May 22, 1981 and I can't remember if I joined the Sunday before or the week after. I do remember Jack Hinson commenting that I had finally "seen the light" when I did join. Actually, Jack shouldn't have been surprised that I was actually coming back to my Baptist roots after a number of years of worshiping and fellowshiping with my Methodist brothers and sisters in Christ.

From then until now, my time at Cullowhee Baptist Church has been a journey of faith and service. I have worshiped with five different full time pastors and a couple or so of interim ministers. These individuals have become my friends over the years. For me it was always with mixed feelings that I watched our pastors come and go.

I have unique memories about each pastor...from Jack Hinson's humor and role-playing in the pulpit to Joe Yelton's sermon on the ministry of green beans and his "If I'm lying, I'm dying" statements of facts, to Mike Vanzura's imagery of dance in our faith journey and references to movies in almost every sermon to Jeffrey and Tonya's passion for missions and children.

I have been mentored and nurtured by strong lay women of faith—Annie Hoyle, Wilma Cosper, Polly Rice, Jane Mitchell, Gladys Parker, Cathie Clayton, Irene Hooper. I have been mentored and nurtured by strong lay men of faith--Jack Barnett, Elmer Hooper, Gene Vosecky, and James Dooley.

I have watched Cullowhee Baptist Church transition from a Southern Baptist Convention (SBC) church to a Cooperative Baptist Fellowship (CBF) church. I have been privileged to serve on three pastoral search committees and to serve as Diaconate Chair on three occasions.

I've enjoyed the unique talents of choir directors—Sara Hinson, Corrine Yelton, Tim Stiles, Terri Ducker, Anne Lough, James Dooley, and Steve Baxley—over the years. For me it has always been about making a joyful noise, and every director has tolerated me with grace.

My children and I have benefited from the talents of our youth directors—Wanda Kidd, Tom Lord, Todd Murdoch, and so many lay persons who served in this capacity. From clowning in Ocean City (ask Eric) to giving a birthday party for Jesus in West Virginia to "beauty" contests at the beach (ask Elizabeth), our youth has laughed and worshiped and served through the years.

I've been blessed by the presence of so many college students through the years. Young people who sojourned with us for awhile and are now scattered far and wide being a presence for Christ in their chosen communities.

I can remember the time when Miss Annie monitored our finances when the finances weren't always so good and I can remember the very few times Cullowhee Baptist ever went into debt to purchase something.

More than anything, I remember that CBC is my church family and through their love and grace I continue my Christian journey.

Harod Dean & Shirley Smith

JoAnne Sutton

Some Excerpts From Member Interviews

A Message from the interviewer, Nicole Jarosinski

I grew up in Wisconsin, moved to Charlotte in middle school, and enrolled at Western Carolina University for college. The scenery and culture in the mountains were so different from what I experienced in Charlotte that I didn't want to leave when school was over. After graduation I stayed in Cullowhee and tried to make a life here. Eventually I went back to school for a Master's Degree in English composition and rhetoric, and I'm finishing that program as this book goes to publication.

My involvement with this book came about through a chance encounter one Saturday morning in June. I drove past some kids washing cars and decided it had been far too long since my little Saturn was last cleaned. On the way home I pulled into the parking lot where the kids were working. The youth and Jeffrey set to scrubbing with brushes and sponges, and I struck up a conversation with two mothers. While chatting I was introduced to Tonya. I told her that I was a graduate student starting a writing career and offered my services for any writing tasks the church needed doing. Two days later I received an email from Amy Ammons Garza telling me she was working on a history of Cullowhee Baptist Church and asking if I would like to help. I've always had an interest in history and minored in it at WCU, so I knew in an instant this project was something I wanted to be involved in. Some may call it a happy coincidence, others may call it God's plan, but either way I'm thrilled I could contribute to this book.

Finally and most importantly, I want to thank Amy and everyone I interviewed for their kindness. I've learned so much about the place where I live that I feel like I can now call myself part of the community. This congregation is the most welcoming group of people I've ever had the pleasure of working with, and I haven't felt such a strong sense of community since I first left my hometown. You all have helped me as much as if not more than, I have helped you. Again, thank you. ■

The interviews in their entirety can be found in the History Room of Cullowhee Baptist Church.

In 1967 the church replaced the orignial stained-glass windows with the beautiful stained glass which now adorns our santurary. In 1987, the old stained glass was made into angels and crosses by Don Wood. The crosses were given to the children for Christmas, and the angels were sold as a building fundraiser. Each of the following interview excerpts will begin with the image of one of these stained-glass windows donated in rememberance of our past members.

Interview
Mr. Winfred Ashe

June 26, 2011
Location: Cullowhee Baptist Church
by Nicole Jarosinski

Nicole: I'm speaking with Winfred Ashe, who is going to share his experiences from Cullowhee Baptist Church. Winfred, how long have you been a member?

Winfred: Approximately 65 years.

N: How did you become a member?

W: Well, I was born in Swain County, in a little town called Judson, North Carolina *[now under Fontana Lake]*. They built the Fontana Dam, and my parents had to move. We moved to Cullowhee in 1943. My parents were Methodists, and I went to the Methodist church in Judson. But when we came to Cullowhee, there were no children my age I associated with that went to the Methodist church. So, I started going to the Baptist church on my own, and I joined the church approximately two years later in 1945. I've been a member approximately 65 years. I hold the church in very high esteem. But I've not always been a good member. I joined in 1945, and I've not been a regular member all of the time, but the past about 12 years I've been here virtually every Sunday after I retired. In the early years all of our neighbors and their children went to the Baptist church. They were real influential in me becoming a member of the Baptist church.

Reverend Osborne became pastor in about 1945, I believe, and the person who impressed me most, and had the most to do with my spiritual relationship with the church was the pastor's wife, Mrs. Osborne. They were a very young couple. Mrs. Osborne taught our Sunday school class in the room just adjoining this on the same floor. She was also a school teacher. Through her teachings, I became more and more interested in the church...when I was about 14 years old. I've always remembered her, and 30 years later she came back, and brought one of her children to Western for the summer school, and I had an opportunity to thank her for what she had done for me. I don't know if she was surprised or not, but she was grateful that I did mention it to her. So that's one of the early experiences that I had.

Some of the people in the community that I looked up to all my life were members of the church. One person in particular, George Crawford Sr., was one of the influential leaders of the church and the community. I learned so much from him. One who only died recently, Mrs. Gladys Parker, who was, if there ever was a saint in Cullowhee...why she was one. I've looked up to her all my life. I tried to pattern my life after her, knowing I couldn't achieve what she's done, but it would be something to try to achieve. Over the years we've had many pastors, and our current ones are...well,

I'd put them at the top of the list. Tonya and Jeffrey are just so friendly, and Tonya has a personality not many people have. She can relate with anybody. So I have really enjoyed the last 10 or 12 years of coming to Cullowhee Baptist more than the previous years, I guess because I've had more time to spend with the church, and I have been a deacon for one four-year term.

N. What was it that Gladys Parker did that made her a saint for you?
W: Well, she was an inspiration to the community. If Gladys Parker did it, why it was all right. I just hold her in such high reverence. Another person who I hold in high esteem was another teacher named Lucy Brown. Now, her grandson is one of the deacons at the church today, Matt Brown. And her son, Manley Brown, I knew him growing up. Lucy was a very humble person, but she was so knowledgeable about the Bible and about church. She was an excellent school and Sunday School teacher, and they'd always call on her for helping in any way in the church. Sometimes when the preacher was gone, she would fill the pulpit for him. She did a great job, but the unfortunate thing about Lucy was that she died of cancer at such an early age. I was talking to Matt just the other day, and they have a daughter now and they named her Lucy after her great grandmother, which I told 'em I thought was wonderful. But she died at a very early age, and Matt wasn't born then. He didn't get to see her. She was such an inspiration for the church.

N: What do you look forward to every year either currently or when you were younger?
W: Well, we have this group that works with a leader that's paid by the county in building ramps for people that are disadvantaged and handicapped and in need of being able to get into their building, their homes, with the aid of a wheel chair and not having to go up steps. Our leader in this is Dr. Pelham Thomas, I don't know whether you know him or not, but he's been the leader since it was organized, I think, and he just does a wonderful job of keeping things organized. Of course it's a nonpayment thing for us, but you get so much out of it. I told Dr. Thomas, "If the people that we built the ramps for enjoyed it as much as we enjoyed doing the work, why they really enjoyed it." We just look forward to that several times a year, maybe once a month through the warmer months of the year. Dr. Thomas has been the leader all the way through and of course he's been my Sunday school teacher and a leader that way. He's done so many wonderful things. He does something all the time for the church. He's one of the ones I'd like to praise who are still here.

N: Do you remember any revivals? Did they have any big revivals here?
W: Why I'll say. When I was growing up, and it's been many many years since they've had revivals here, but they usually lasted a week. And it'd be a lot of people saved and that sort of things. When it would get going real good sometimes they wouldn't cut it off at the end of the week—it'd run on several more nights.

N: I just have to ask since this church [was] a Southern Baptist and for a long time Southern Baptists were against dancing, how did that work out at the revival?

W: Well, all right, let me tell you a little story about that. When I was about maybe 16 years old, the veterans were coming back from World War Two and some of 'em who had been wounded were housed in Asheville. They brought them to Breese Gym, which is the rock gymnasium just up the road here, for a dance on Saturday night. The college girls were supposed to dance with them and they said they were lectured real close cuz if the boys say, "Well let's go for a walk," they'd say, "We're not expected to leave the room." But, the thing I wanted to tell you the most was about the president of the college at that time was Dr. Hunter, and he sang in the choir. One of the very few Baptist presidents we've had since I've been in Cullowhee. On the Sunday morning after the dance, why Reverend Osborne got up and in his sermon he says. "You know, I feel so sad today." He says, "Of all the things that could have happened in Cullowhee, they had a DANCE last night." And Dr. Hunter just kinda held his head down and looked at the floor.

N: What do you remember most about previous pastors? You mentioned the Osbornes.

W: Well, I remember Osborne real well and his wife more especially than him. I do remember Dr. Yelton. He was one fine person. I just assumed him to be, from the time he was born, he was intended to be a preacher. But I got to know him pretty well and he said, "You know, in my younger life – " and he was still a young man, but he said, "in my younger life I was kinda wild." He said, "I drank a lot and carried on like I shouldn't have," one thing and another. When he came to school, here a well-known family in the community—Harry Duke and Sue Duke—were ardent members of the church and they just more or less took him under their wing. He said they were his parents-in-residence while he was here, and apparently they did a whole lot to change his life. He done such a wonderful job here. Now his church is in Candler.

N: How do you feel about the Vickerys?

W: Well, I hold 'em in very high esteem. They were very young as pastors when they came here. I was fortunate in being able to welcome them when they came to the parsonage, when they first moved. And they just fit in right with the community. Basically at heart they're missionaries, and I don't know if sometime if the opportunity arrives they may follow that, but I hope it's not in my lifetime at least. But they're wonderful people. And Tonya, you know as good as I do, after you've talked to her five minutes, why you feel like you've been a friend for life. And of course Jeffrey has a good personality too, but she's just tops. And Jeffrey, he's active on these ramp buildings. He knows what to do and he just gets right in and just moves on with it.

N: Can you tell me about when they first arrived and issues with her being a woman pastor 'cuz I understand some of the other churches around here did not like that.

W: Well, it was certainly not a issue with the congregation here at this church, but they have what they call the Tuckaseigee Baptist Association which has been in effect here in Jackson County for years. They were opposed to it. And of course,

Tonya and Jeffrey both tried to talk to 'em about it and Tonya more especially. I think maybe they kinda got received a little bit rudely, but it's never been an issue within our church. It did have an effect on some of the churches around. Some of the churches withdrew from the Tuckaseigee Baptist Association because of their resentment to them. Now, in my opinion, and it even goes back to the Bible, women can preach just as good as men can. On Saturday night now, my wife and I—my wife who's not able to attend church—we listen to this program in South Carolina, where this woman preaches ever Saturday night. We just look forward to it from one time to another. And I always look forward to the days that Tonya preaches. She fits in so good with the community. So I think it's real unfortunate that Tuckaseigee Baptist Association had that opinion to start with. Now, I'm not aware of what's communicated lately, but I think it has changed to a great extent. I'm not sure whether they're all the way over it yet or not. But anyway, Cullowhee will survive with or without.

N: What was a significant moment in time for you as a member that sticks out?
W: Well I guess if I had to come up with one significant time, it was when I joined the church. They have the same baptistery as they did 65 years ago. I remember walking to the front before I was baptized that day, and I remember walking downstairs underneath it. Professor Stillwell, who taught one of the Sunday school classes, was walking by and he says, "I see there's going to be a baptism today because the water's aleakin' out through the ceiling." I can vividly see it in my mind as if it happened yesterday. It was during the winter months because the preacher and his wife took me home after the service. You know I got my clothes wet and they let me get changed. They said they didn't want to take any chance of me catching the cold. I thought that was awfully thoughtful of them.

...Oh, there's one person who I want to tell you about—Fred Dills. His wife still goes to this church here, Thelma Dills, He was one of the most wonderful people I've ever met. We would meet at Burger King during the week, you know, and have breakfast. He was a member of the East LaPorte Lodge of which I've been a member for almost 60 years. We just had so much in common. He was a person who would have you laughing in five minutes. He was in my opinion, one of the saints at this church. Now he's just been dead about five or six years something like that. Everbody liked him, and I think about him almost every day because he was such a close friend and the church and lodge and all.

N: If you would like to, lastly, if you want to share your own conversion story, just because you mentioned it. Or how that happened.
W: How that happened? Well, I had gone to vacation bible school and Mrs. Osborne was a teacher at that time. I was very shy at that time. I was about 13 or 14 years old. And I didn't go with the group. I had an urge to, but I didn't. Later on Mrs. Osborne, sometime about Christmastime, in her Sunday school class, she ask how many had not been converted, and of course I had to raise my hand. And she says, "I'm so surprised at you. Have you ever thought about it?" I said, "I think about it and pray about it

every night just about." And she says, "Well, now we're gonna do something about that." She helped me so much, and I mean it just felt like a weight had been lifted from me. I believe the day that she talked to me about it she says, "Now I'm not going to tell you to do this today. But the first time you get the urge, at the end of the service you come on up." And I came up that day. And I was so, so happy. She was so happy she cried. Of course a lot of people didn't know that she had been involved that much, but she was so instrumental. That was really the happiest time I guess. I talked with my mother, who was a very religious person—of course they were Methodists and had no thought of changing—I talked to her about it a little bit before I joined and she said, "They basically really have the same beliefs." And she said, "It's my fault that you didn't stay in the Methodist church. I'm just happy you're gonna be a member." So I thought was really good advice cuz a lot of parents mighta not had that attitude.

N: I want to thank you so much for your time and allowing me to interview you.
W: Wanted to mention my admiration for Dr. Gene Vosecky, Sunday School instructor and brother in the Lodge. My message to future members: join early and stay in the church.

Interview: Beth and Steve Baxley

July 18, 2011
by Nicole Jarosinski

N: First of all, how did you two come to join the church? What made you choose Cullowhee Baptist?
B: Well, we moved here in 1980 and we visited Cullowhee Baptist when Jack Hinson was pastor. I remember when we were leaving Jack shook our hand and said, "I would love to come visit you all," which was really touching. And he did come over that week. He was just such a wonderful, genuine, delightful person, so we continued to go.

S: We were there for about three years and we'd already started teaching and I had started singing in the choir, and then we realized that we'd never really joined. What Jack did was a big influence. We liked him and his messages really spoke to us. And Annie Hoyle, who was the Sunday school director at that time, befriended us. Those friendships really made the difference.
B: Annie Hoyle was a great lady of our church. She had been a teacher for probably 50 years, when schools were one-room classrooms. She never had

children of her own, but she took us in and I remember after we had been going about six months she said one day, "Beth, would you like to help out with the kindergarten Sunday school group?" I said sure, and the next thing I knew I was listed as the teacher. That's how I ended up being a Sunday school teacher. I found out I loved it, and I think Annie knew I would love it. She had her ways, didn't she. She was the treasurer for a long time.

S: She had her own treasury system, which took a while for people to figure out after she wasn't in that position any longer.

N: What did she do for you that made her so dear?

B: I got really close to her in a small study group, and I started visiting her at her home. She got to be a friend and confidante, somebody who I could talk with. She was so kind in listening and sharing her wisdom with me.

S: She was really good with Lauren, who was two at the time, and that meant a lot to us. There were times I would go over and hang out in her yard because we lived on campus at the time. I was working in residential living and so we were always in apartments.

B: She had a magic backyard. It had little groves of trees and these little concrete animals. Lauren was enchanted with it. It was like a secret garden. That's a sweet memory of her. She was just like a grandmother, a spiritual grandmother. I do remember when our church was interviewing after Jack Hinson left to become the hospital chaplain, a story about the deacons interviewing Joe Yelton. They were letting him know what our church was like, so they shared some specific information, and at one point one of the deacons said, "And now we need to share with you about our Annie." They were really just letting him know that this lady had her own way of doing things and that was the way she did it. He just needed to understand the way Annie worked.

N: Can you tell me about any camping trips that really stand out?

S: It was a great group at that time who went camping. Has anybody talked about Bill Mincey and the bear? That was a great trip. I remember on that same trip Jeremy, one of Bill and Bonnie's kids, loved cheese puffs. And if you go camping over in Cade's Cove there's skunks everywhere that just come right up into the campsite. So we'd be sitting around the campfire after eating dinner and the skunks would be underneath our chairs and running around and we'd throw them cheese puffs every once in a while to keep them happy.

B: But we did caution the kids, "Don't move." And we never got sprayed.

S: One of our other places to go to was up in Virginia at Bear Tree. It's part of the Jefferson National Forest, near Damascus. It was a neat place to go if you're into camping and hiking because the Appalachian Trail is close by and the Virginia Creeper Trail, also. At the time Etheree's husband Paul had started hiking the Appalachian Trail in sections. On one trip we took there, he was going to hike the section around the campground and Etheree was going to meet him at one point to pick him up. When she got there he wasn't there and it got dark and she was still waiting for him. Of course back at the campground we didn't know what was going on. We went to sleep and they still hadn't come back. Then the next morning they were there. I think he had misjudged how long the trip was going to take.

B: And his flashlight battery had gone out.

S: So he was hiking the AT and couldn't see where he was going. We made a big joke about Paul losing his sight on the road to Damascus just like Saul did.

B: There were about eight families and lots of kids in that group were great friends with each other. We would just sit around that campfire and sing, and of course the cooking was fantastic. And telling stories. Millions of stories. I think that was the closest we've ever been to any group. It's amazing how much you bond when you camp together. And Etheree organized it all. She was THE quintessential organizer. She could get five times more done in a day than anybody I've ever seen. Of course people age, the kids aged, and the camping thing kind of went by the wayside. But for about 12 years that was really special.

S: I can remember the only time we got Joe and Corrine to go with us to Gatlinburg to a commercial campground.

B: Which was very upscale compared to the rest of the campgrounds we stayed in.

S: I remember just laughing when Joe had gone out and gotten his camping gear. They erected this huge tent.

B: Oh, it was as big as this room.

S: And they got electricity and heat. I think they had television. We really ragged them.

B: But you know they were being very sportsmanlike to do that because they were not campers. They really hung in there with us.

N: Did you start the Wednesday night meals?

S: It started out as a small informal prayer meeting, and when we added the meal we were getting the food from a local restaurant. Barrett's closed, and I may have been the first cook after that. For two or three years I did the Wednesday night meal. We had a rotation of stuff we did over a six-week period. Barbeque one night, and chicken a la king the next week. That was when food service on campus was run by Western, it wasn't Aramark. I had a deal with them about buying entrees, and I would make whatever else went with it. It was really easy to put together. Lauren and I had a great time doing it together. I think that's why she likes to cook so much. It's where I introduced the church to the infamous snow caps. It's this recipe where you slice hotdogs down the middle and you put mashed potatoes on top and cheese on top of that and bake them in the oven. They had a mixed reception by the church.

B: The students loved them. They insisted on Steve making them once a month.

S: That was one of the things in rotation. We were always introducing a new group of people to snow caps. I cooked a few years until my job changed and I really didn't have the flexibility. There were a few people who were regular cooks after that.

N: So how did you become choir director, Steve?

S: Well, let's see. I had always sung since I was little. My dad was choir director from time to time in the churches we attended growing up. I quit singing for a few years but started back after we came to Cullowhee Baptist Church. It would have been 12 or 13 years ago. James Dooley retired [as choir director], and I was asked to serve as interim while they did a search. I didn't know anything about directing at all. Thank goodness for James and Barbara. They know so much and are so professional about music; they were so helpful. I had sung all my life but I didn't know anything about reading music. Nothing. So I agreed to do it but asked James if he would help and give me some pointers. It was a trial by fire because I never had to pick out music before. I kinda knew how Dad had done things. One of the things I do that he did, he would pencil in the hymnal the date that he used a particular hymn. I do the same thing; I date songs when I use them to keep track. And if you look at the grey hymnal that I use, I've used it for so long now I'm running out of room for some hymns. I'll never forget after the first Sunday of worship I asked James, "What advice can you give me?" And he said, "Well, the first thing is that you're directing backwards." I'd always been sitting out looking at a director so I hadn't thought about it; the standpoint of the director is reversed. James would give me suggestions in such a great way that I never felt like I didn't know what I was doing or I was terrible. I've always thought there must be days he's biting his tongue but I can't tell at all. Anyway I was able to fill in as interim for several months, and then they selected Terri Ducker to be the director. She was a member of our church and had a much better music background than I did. But I enjoyed it so much that I decided I wanted to learn more about it in case I ever had an opportunity to do it again. So I went back to the choir but I took some courses at Western. I took music theory, voice lessons, conducting, and concert choir so that I could get rudiments of music. Then, when Terri left, they asked me to be the interim director again and I've been doing that for 11 years now. They've never officially made me director. They dropped the "interim" in the bulletin at some point so maybe that's official.

B: Nobody knows when Steve started but they decided that he had probably been music director for 500 Sundays and they threw this great party with these hilarious what's-that-tune games. It was a great night. It was dinner, and these games, and a little bit of a roast, and everybody letting him know how much they appreciated him. It was really fun and all the former pastors came.

N: James Dooley wanted me to ask you about including the young people in the choir, if that was a decision other than getting a bigger choir.

S: I don't know that it was really a planned thing, but almost four years ago Tonya and Jeffrey asked me about working with the kids on Wednesday night. They started M&Ms—Music and Missions—with the elementary kids. My part was music. I remember I didn't even really want to do it because I didn't know anything about how you're supposed to do music with kids. So I did what I do with adults. We did a lot of the camp song kind of things, the stuff we all learned growing up, but I didn't want to just do that. I wanted to sing things out of the choral music tradition. So we would occasionally have them do pieces like that. Sometimes it might have a solo part. And I would find pieces they could sing with the adults. I don't remember a point where I said, "Why don't you all start singing in the adult choir." I think that as the girls got older they wanted to keep singing. It was great for them to do that and have that experience, and nobody said not to do it. I think they really enjoy it and they're learning some things about singing in a group, some good technique. As you can tell I'm not a stickler for real disciplined choir etiquette. I hear from other people sometimes, "Can you work with them a bit about standing straight?" I haven't worried about that too much.

B: They really are doing well. They're sweet kids.

S: I like the sound they bring to the group. It adds to worship and gives them a place to be a part of worship, rather than just sitting there listening. I'm glad it's worked out the way it has.

N: Would either of you like to give a message to future members?

B: You find a family when you come to our church and that's been very precious to me.

S: A real strength of the church is people living out their faith. Individual members do it in their own way. I think there's a lot of people in the church who live out their faith day to day in a quiet way where they're serving other people or serving the church. And nobody makes a big deal out of it, but it all comes together to form the community. It's people downstairs during worship taking care of kids; you don't necessarily know exactly who they are unless you see their name in the bulletin. Or that Cathie Clayton for as long as anybody can remember has made the grape juice for communion. All those little things together make the community. My message would be for people to find that place. There's a role everybody has, whatever it is. Find that and live it out.

B: That reminds me of a great story Joe Yelton told. In a church he used to pastor, there was a woman who came to him one day and said, "I don't have any talents, I really don't have anything to offer, and I feel bad that I don't have any contribution in this church." Joe asked her, "Well, what do you do well?" She just thought for the longest time and finally said, "You know, I make really good green beans." And he said, "That's it right there." So the next time they had a covered dish she brought her green beans, which really were fabulous and people raved about them. Ever after that, her ministry was the green-bean ministry. If a family was sick, if there was a funeral, anything where there was a need for food, she was there with her fabulous green beans. Joe used that story to illustrate it doesn't have to be something that we think of as being this great talent. It's just that we are all parts of the body of Christ and the way the community is taken care of is everybody doing what God brings them to. Another thing is Robert Lanning. Many years ago he started calling people anytime they had a birthday or anniversary. He's done that now for about 30 years and everybody knows him as the Happy Birthday Guy. And it's really a sweet thing when you have a birthday or anniversary you know you're gonna get a call from Robert. About 10 years ago on his birthday we did a big surprise party for him being our birthday minister. Isn't that sweet? I just love that.

N: What do you look forward to every year besides the Birthday Guy?

B: I always look forward to communion the first Sunday of the month. We started doing cake auctions a couple years ago and those are hilarious. People will bid hundreds of dollars on a cake to raise money for ministries. And sometimes it's not even a church ministry. It may be something related to a community effort.
S: Definitely Advent and Lent, particularly as minister of music. We started shifting to the liturgical calendar with Mike Vanzura. It's a lot of work but I always look forward to services those two times of year. Also I look forward to the times when there's a group working together on something. Like the Saturday before students come back when we get together and make ice cream to serve at Valley Ballyhoo. I always look forward to those to participate in.

N: My last question is what was a significant moment for you as a member?
B: When our daughter was baptized. That was really special to see her baptized in our church. And I remember something that really stands out as being hilarious. Joe Yelton was doing a Bible study one Wednesday night. Back then there was a rest home in Cullowhee called Community Care, and it was primarily people who were mentally handicapped that lived there. There were quite a few of those folks who went to our church and they were very involved in worship service and Wednesday nights. There was this one darling little guy who's name was Billy West, and Billy loved to come Wednesday nights and he would always fall asleep as soon as Joe started doing Bible study. Billy's head would just nod over and he'd jerk up every so often, but mostly he slept through the Bible study. One night during the study Joe said, "I say to you, WAKE UP!" and pounded his fist on the table. Billy shot up saying, "I'm awake!" We all just died laughing.
S: For me there's no one big event. I can think of little things that mean a lot to me. Anytime we have a baby dedication. That symbol of welcoming a baby into the community and acknowledging our responsibility towards that child. Communion, when we do candlelight communion at Christmastime; the juxtaposition of Christ's birth and death at the same service and all that means. The first Sunday of the month when I know Cathie's not in choir because she's getting communion ready with her grape juice.
B: And the little kids after communion. Every month they pick up all the little communion cups and the thrill of the day is to drink the rest of the communion grape juice and eat the bread. It's this little ritual they delight in. They're ready as soon as the service is over.
S: I remember when Tracy Vanzura's dad passed away. There was a group of us who said we need to hop in the car and drive down to South Carolina and go be there to visit. It's those things that really stick out to me.

Themla and Fred Dills

Interview: Sue and Baxter Wood

Date: July 6, 2011
by Nicole Jarosinski

N: How did you two first come to join the church?
S: We were living in Cullowhee. We had married and gotten us an apartment.
B: We were students at the university.
S: We weren't that far from home but we wanted to go to church here.

N: Was there a big crowd that went to church at that time?
S: Yeah, a lot of students because there wasn't all of the other things to do in Cullowhee. It was a full house.
B: They used to have a choir over there that was absolutely unbelievable. They'd fill that choir loft. In 1969 I was chairman of the board of deacons, and our pastor resigned. We had an interim pastor, Dr. Jimmy Day, and if you weren't there before church time, you couldn't get a seat. That church was filled every Sunday.
S: We had folding chairs carried out.
B: Chairs down the aisle, down the side, and on the sides of the pulpit, that whole area up there. It was filled and that was every Sunday that Dr. Jimmy Day was here. Then we got a new pastor and he continued to pretty much fill it.

N: Would you say the choir used to be a bragging point?
B: Oh yes. I would say there was no choir certainly within the Tuckaseigee Baptist Association that was comparable to it, that had the musical knowledge.

1990

Back in these outlying churches they were more gospel-music type.
S: Southern gospel. What they did was they probably didn't practice. Anybody who wanted to sit in the choir they'd go sit in the choir. And they'd say, "Okay, take your books, page 230." So they'd all open their books to see what 230 was and that's what they'd sing. But they had good voices so they got their points across.
B: I grew up in that type of church where you had a quartet or maybe eight people who'd sing, but as far as any robes and practice and all that.. there just wasn't. And a lot of churches didn't have what they'd call a choir. Sue grew up in that kind of church, too.
S: We had a...he wasn't called a choir director...he was maybe the Sunday school superintendent, and would take care of the music. A lot of the churches didn't have an organ. Most of them had pianos, but not organs. Even if you had an organ you didn't have anybody in church that knew how to play it. That was the problem with getting an organ. And sometimes the person playing the piano didn't have any music. They played by ear.

It was a different world back then.

B: You may know Cullowhee Baptist Church was paid for mostly by the State Baptist Convention when this new church was built. In 1928 it cost $33,000. The only reason I know is I was coordinator of a quarter-million dollar improvement in 2000, and I went back in the church records and saw what the difference was.

S: One thing, I know you've seen where the church was organized in 1821. Baxter's great great grandfather, Henry Wood, was one of the founders. Baxter and our son are the only two descendants of the founding fathers who still have the last names. There are other people that are descendants, but they don't have the last name of the fathers.

B: That's what we were told at the 175th anniversary.

N: When you came back from Virginia, how did you feel you had been accepted by the church?

S: You're family, honey. Everybody in that church like Pokey Watson and Jean Mincey, they watched our kids grow up. They were special to 'em. When our daughter got married I think everybody in the church was at that wedding. You can't image how many people. And you would see 'em, trying to get your lists made out, and they'd say "Oh, I can't wait till Deborah's wedding!" And I'd think, is their name on the list? We'll have to go and put their name on the list. So we sent them all invitations to it. We said we'll have them all there. It's home any way you look at it. And we've done about every job in the church until we got too old.

N: What stands out to you about Cullowhee Baptist?

S: It's home. You just feel home. We've gone to a few other churches, gone to a church where we knew everybody in there, but it wasn't home. It just did not have the feeling of home.

N: Has there been anybody in your time in the church who has meant the most to you?

B: Well a great many that I admired; I'm sure I'll leave out someone. Dean Harrill, Dr. Smith, there's several. Dr. Vosecky, Jack Barnett....

S: You see those stained glass doors on the baptistery? Jack Barnett did those.

B: Miss Hunter. Jean Mincey's mother; you never had to guess where she stood or what she thought. She'd tell you. And she wouldn't hesitate to tell the preacher what she thought, either. Maude Sherrill; she was a pillar in that church.

N: I've been asking a lot of people to tell me about the revivals they had here.

S: I don't remember any at Cullowhee Baptist Church as a child because we weren't going then, but we used to go to them at Old Savannah all the time. If you had a good one going, people would come from everywhere they could to get to it. And we walked. I mean there was no way of getting there except you walked from your house to the church.

B: I was trying to remember one. Dr. Fred Forrester. He's the only one I could think of that you would call an evangelical preacher. He was here in the 30s and went out to different churches and had revivals. This was a big thing, a revival in the fall of the year after everything had been taken care of. It was primarily an agrarian society in which we grew up, and when everything was taken care of, they would have revivals. They would try not to overlap.

N: Can you walk me through a typical day for a revival?

S: Well everybody worked on farms and they'd work all day. At that time of year it was corn gathering time, and the men would get all of that done and they'd have supper and then they'd go to church. It was that type of thing. Now I know that in our church when I was growing up, the women, the ones that were not working on a job or something, they would meet at the church for a prayer service. Every day they had a prayer service at the church.

B: They'd start 'em on a Sunday night and sometimes they would run for two weeks if you got a real fireball preacher. Usually it was a week.

S: It was a different type of revival by the time we got back here to Cullowhee Baptist.

B: They would invite a speaker to come in for about three nights. Cullowhee was a more subdued, formal thing. It was a different atmosphere. I grew up where these mostly women, I don't remember ever seeing any men do it, but a lot of these women would get up and just shout all over the church.

S: I have seen people who could hardly walk, but honey that spirit hit them and they could jump across benches. I mean they would just glide. You could feel the spirit because you knew when they got it. My daddy would always say, "Well, Aunt Sally will probably be shoutin' tonight." Of course I'd be big-eyed, waiting to see if Aunt Sally was going to dance.

B: Where I grew up at Balsam Grove Baptist there were three or four women that you could guarantee every night they were gonna shout.

S: There was nothing different about it. Everybody expected it and said, "They're just feeling the spirit. They've really got the spirit." Of course the preacher liked it because it made his sermons more energetic.

N: Is there something you look forward to every year?

S: Ten years ago at least we had one of the best times, even though it was a lot of hard work. We had a bazaar. It was so organized that they had one room where they had the country store, one room where you had the linens, one room where you had Christmas things. We made over $10,000 that year. We had flea market items. We had baked goods. But everybody worked. We did it for two or three years but the first one was the big one. It was enjoyable; it was hard work, but everybody had a good time. And then the last one we had was after Ed and Carolyn [Robison] started coming to our church because he's the one we teased about letting that woman steal that couch. We had everything that was yard-sale items outside under a tent, and this woman came up there looking at a couch they had. Ed and Pat [Angel] were there and they said, "We'll deliver it for you if you want it." It wasn't but $25. She said, "Well, I'll think about it. I'll come back." So she went inside the building and looked around at all the other stuff. She came back out and told us, "I'll take that couch." And they said, "It'll be $25." She said, "Oh, I paid the lady inside," and they said okay. So they loaded up that couch on their truck and took it home for her then came back.

Somebody asked Mary Jo, "Did that woman give you $25 for that couch?" And she said, "Nobody paid me for a couch." They said, "Well, maybe it was Brenda." So they called her and Brenda said, "No, nobody gave me any money." We teased them for a long time about letting a woman steal the couch from them and they delivered it for her. The funny part about it was we'd a give it to her if she was hard-up and needed it that bad.

N: Do you have any message you'd like to give to future members of Cullowhee Baptist?

S: I have to tell people that you got to go where you're comfortable. If you go in that church and you don't feel comfortable, then go somewhere else. 'Cuz God doesn't want you to have a forced religion. It's open. It's yours. So if you feel comfortable going to that church and the people that speak you and you think well I believe I could make a difference here, I think God called me to come here. And that would be the thing because there are too many churches now that you're bound to find one.

Interview: Stedman Mitchell

Date: July 24, 2011
by Nicole Jarosinski

N: So Stedman, how did you first come to join the church?

S: I bought a farm in 1939 up in Speedwell. I was in the produce business, went out of that and went into farming and producing milk for sale. While I was there, my wife and I built a little house. We moved into that in 1942, and the first Sunday we were up there we came down to the Baptist church. A man and his wife, Preston Smith and Zula, followed us home after church and they invited us to become members. Course we were Baptists, had been all our lives. And that's the way we started going to the Baptist church in Cullowhee.

1990

N: What do you remember most about your time in Cullowhee Baptist Church?

S: One of my big memories is way back yonder the choir that we had was developed by Preston Smith and his wife Zula. They got that choir up close to 50 members. They had about six or eight couples and older members, but most of them were students. That's one of the highlights. And of course being in charge of raising funds a couple times for development of the church. Our church was just so standstill. After Joe Yelton left, we were just absolutely standing still. So I sold a little property and picked up a little money and started fundraising. We had all these things planned but nobody would do anything about it.

N: What kinds of things?
S: Reworking bathrooms, for instance. And bringing the kitchen up to a point that wasn't illegal. You gotta have certain standards, and we were way behind on a lot of that stuff. We put in a new water system, new plumbing, new electricity upstairs. We just rebuilt the church. I started it with $10,000, and it woke 'em up. You wouldn't believe the things people came together and did. We had yard sales; I mean we had good furniture piled all over everything. I mean we sold stuff you wouldn't believe you'd bring to a yard sale.

In the late 40s when Germany retreated, people in the Balkan countries like Latvia, Lithuania, Estonia, they just loaded up on these trains and followed the Germans back rather than face the Russians. Germany had been beaten down, they were out of business as far as the war and fighting, but they set up camps there for all these people who didn't want to face the Russians. We got word and our church made a request to take on a family out of the camps, and I'm proud of that. We all got together and we talked about this thing, and I went and handled it. Nobody really had the nerve...I didn't have the nerve either, but when they got to looking at me, I volunteered to take care of a family with the church's help. And they were a great help after it got started. But they needed somebody to start it. Well I didn't have a house to put the family in, so I built a house in Speedwell on that farm I had there, a log house. It really wasn't a place that you should move a family into, but we felt it was better than what they had over there. So we got that family and the church got in behind it and we kept the family there until they could get their feet on the ground.

The father's name was Arnold Usis. He was a Baptist minister in Latvia, so he fit right in with our program. There were his wife, his sister, and three teenage boys—one of those boys was a deaf mute. Of course they couldn't even shop for themselves. Arnold could speak English. He spoke better English than I did, really. But the rest of the family spoke no English. So ordering food and stuff like that, I would have to go or somebody would have to go with 'em to the grocery store. I was a supervisor of a second farm in my spare time, and I gave Arnold a job over there as a common laborer. He was an educated person, but common laborer was the only thing that I could offer him.

So he worked over there and earned enough to buy his groceries and stuff. I bought him a cow. And they could do anything with milk. You can't believe the things they did with a couple gallons of milk a day. Unbelievable. They made the prettiest butter you ever saw. They made all kinds of puddings and stuff like that. They got 'em a hog, fed it, and killed it for the meat, then smoked the meat in a barrel. I'd never heard of any such thing. But they were workers, by the grace of God. They worked day and night. Of course, we knew they weren't real happy. In the first place, the country people up the road up there wouldn't even speak to 'em cause they were foreigners. And see, we don't remember anything about that period, but that was all over the United States really. Specially country people. They just wouldn't have anything to do with 'em. "Not our kind of folks. "They went through that period, which is something... not much you can do. Arnold was invited to several Baptist churches to conduct a service, which was great. And it was something these folks had never heard of. He was smart. He was a good preacher. But he was corresponding with a group up north; he found some folks up there he knew during this camp or maybe at home in Latvia. And they were corresponding with one another. After about a year and a half or two years, he wanted to move his family up there, which was great with us. So they they moved up there.

A lot of people chipped in and helped them, but one of the nice things in my part of it was two or three years maybe after that, somebody came to my front door one afternoon. I went out there and I didn't recognize the man, and it was one of these boys and he came by to say hello to me. He was headed to Jacksonville, Florida, to get on a boat, to put in two years on the boat as a dentist. He was on a program where you put in two years in service and the government would mark off what you owe them in education. And that's what he had done. He sat here and we talked about what the family was doing. His father Arnold was an interpreter for the whole area around where they moved to. His mother was a janitress in some banks. The deaf mute was working in typesetting. The other kid was still in school. They had just done great. I had dreaded, I had felt like I hadn't done as much for them, I couldn't afford to do more as they might have expected, but after talking to this boy about how they all turned out, I felt pretty good about it. I haven't heard from 'em since. I'd like to know what happened in these years gone by.

Everybody did a beautiful job.

N: What stands out to you about Cullowhee Baptist Church or the people in it? Could you characterize them?

S: They're just a great group of people to work with. My wife, she lived here with me for almost two years not knowing half the time where she was, wanting to get out and go home. Alzheimer's. It's a terrible thing. But the way people in the church helped us, and so many of them brought us food knowing that we're having a tough time, organizing everything I was looking after then. And you don't know what to do or what not to do. But that support. And they've done all the people like that. If they knew that you needed something they'd try to get it for you or do it for you. Just good people.

Jane Mitchell, 1989

N: What did you look forward to every year?

S: Well, let me see. I love those Christmas programs, the music programs. Another thing I wanted to mention, Etheree Chancellor got together with some folks and she was the kingpin and developed this "Trail of Light." It was a big program. I was in it even as an actor. Amy, and Etheree, and another woman, a costume specialist, worked with them. They developed something there that was unusual and very nice. A lot of people involved with it; they used about all of us. And we had the animals into it. And music, you wouldn't believe the music they brought together. It lasted a few years and of course it just runs out. Everybody seen it and they'd all haul to it. That was one of the highlights of our church in my 40 or 50 years of it. But the highlights were raising that money a time or two and they put me in charge of it for some reason or another. And I was involved in that and of course this family was all over here from Germany. Everybody was involved in those things. Those were some highlights for the church I think that I was involved in somehow.

N: Did you attend any revivals? Could you tell me what they were like?
S: We haven't had any in a long time, but we did have them in the 50s and 60s. Of the activities in the church, those revivals were about the only thing that spiked everybody up and got 'em going. We had one every year. They'd invite some high-powered pastor in to do those revivals. But it was a good thing back then. Our church has always had a problem with new members, getting new members. But we're not the only ones. I think that most university campuses have this problem. They've got 10,000 people right here under their nose to influence. But we're not influencing 'em. And another thing is young couples. That's where the big problem is. Now if you invite a young couple that's just come in here, say for teaching, the first thing they're looking for is someone their own age. But we haven't been able to develop eight or ten of those couples that can have their own tables, their own pews, and things in common.

N: Do you have a message you'd like to say to future church members?
S: Build a group. You might use that as something that might increase interest in the church, to get more young couples who have something in common to stay with the church cuz it's hard to... if one or two comes, where you gonna get another four or five? Unless they stay there and wait for another two or three to come.

Bob and Anne Setzer
Laura, Joel and Steve

E.W. and Catherine Vosecky

Interview: Bonnie Hooper

September 8, 2011
by Nicole Jarosinski

N: Do you remember any fun times with the church from when you were growing up?
B: The choir director, Ruth Hooper, took the younger ones on a camping trip one time, and we camped out all night on Cullowhee Creek. We had a lot of fun together and cooked out on a campfire. We didn't have sleeping bags, but we had quilts and whatnot. We slept on those. Then the next morning we went home. We used to have church-wide picnics up the road from my house on [Toad Road.]. There's a spring and an open place. There were a lot of kids in church when I was growing up and we did a lot of fun together, being together, singing together, and playing together. As youngsters, the church was open a lot for us.

N: Can you tell me about making quilts to fundraise for the fellowship hall?
B: We made many different things for that. Some women quilted, some knitted. Other people couldn't cross stitch so I did that. Harriet Parker, Christine Crawford, and myself made quilts and we hand-quilted them to sell. We made quite a bit of money on our quilts besides all of the other arts and crafts that we did. Now, other ladies in the church participated too. It was the whole group, the older ladies and the younger ladies in the church, doing those sales. We had canned goods that we canned ourselves for sale. That was for the bazaar to redo the fellowship hall. Before I ever got involved there was a group of other older ladies that always did a Christmas bazaar, and it was held at Western. They raised money for things at the church. When we were doing all that work it was a lot of fun because a lot of women were working with us. We sold one quilt for $2,000, a cathedral window quilt. Harriet, Christine, and I made it and it was all handmade with little squares. It was a really beautiful quilt. I think Mike Vanzura bought it for his wife Tracy.

N: What's the very first memory you have about being in church?
B: Being in my Sunday school class. Then we all went to church and the whole group of young people sat on the very back row. There was a guy that would go to sleep every Sunday. Of course that tickled all of us.

N: Is that what started the back row group in church now?
B: I don't think so. The people that I sit with now were not members of the church at the time. For many years, Berter Long sat on the end of that back row. He was an old man. He used to be the postmaster of Cullowhee, and that

was his seat. After he died my husband and I started sitting back there. His daughter Pokie [Lora Watson] goes to church there now. Pokie's son Bill and his wife Bonnie went on a cruise with us. Joe Yelton got it together. A group of us left from Tampa, Florida, to Cancun and Cozumel, Mexico. The boat had the first slot machines we'd ever seen, so another woman and I played the slot machines and we would always laugh and say, "If I win anything I'm gonna give it to the church," but we didn't win. We'd just play a little bit and leave it. Of course we went to the dances every night. It was a good trip. Just to be with that group of people. And they were the older people.

For years Jean Painter and I cooked Wednesday night meals. We enjoyed the time together. It got to the point that I couldn't do it anymore. As you get older, you have to slow down. We would go on Tuesdays and buy groceries. Then on Wednesdays we'd go cook. We always had a big crowd. We used to cook a lot of country meals and they really liked it.

N: What do you look forward to every year?
B: The fellowship dinners that we have because we go into church and we have just a few minutes to greet each other. Then after church it's been so hot lately that everybody just leaves. Then in the winter it's so cold. And Christmas Eve is very special to me to sit in the church and sing Christmas songs. The heart of Christ is in the church then, instead of Santa Claus.

N: What was your happiest moment connected to the church?
B: My wedding was the happiest. Of course I was always happy in the church because we just loved going. We really did. I got married in October 1955 and Roland Pruitt was the minister. It wasn't a big wedding. It was just me and my husband and witnesses, Bill and Shirley Simpson. They were friends of ours. I wanted to be married in the church but I didn't want to have a big wedding.

N: What would you like to say to future members of Cullowhee Baptist?
B: I go to worship and to be with friends and come home having a good feeling. I think that church services are a part of your life. That's my feeling. I would love to see more people attending because it is a good church with a family group of people. And of course it's been here so long that I just feel like it'll always be there.

Kim and Mike Poteet, 1988

Interview: Dr. Jeff Davis

July 10, 2011
by Nicole Jarosinski

Jeff's first recollection with the church was being invited to Bill and Bonnie Mincey's house. Jeff and his wife, Sandy, didn't know anybody and Bill said, "Come on over for dinner." Then Jeff and Sandy were invited to join the choir. They sang long before they became members. In fact, Jeff recalled, "When we joined the church we joined wearing our choir robes." With a wink, Jeff said, "We joined the church for two reasons. One, they had better food than the Methodists. And two, they were more fun than other churches. What got us involved was not the preaching, but because everybody was welcoming and lots of fun.

"Our first trip we camped overnight at Deep Creek. We had a campfire, marshamallows, and our guitars. Sandy was new to camping, so it was a fun way to break her into camping with a group.

"The event I'll always remember was five years ago when Connor decided to get baptized and nobody told me. They planned it, everybody knew, and all it said in the bulletin was that someone was gonna be baptized. Next thing I knew Tonya said, 'And now Connor Davis will come and be baptized.' Connor was smiling and laughing and Tonya was beaming. I had no clue until he walked into the water that he was going to be baptized that day."

Jeff felt he belonged in this church because it had a gospel of grace, mercy, and fellowship. People lived what they preached.

"Members made sure we were all taking care of each other. If you ever needed something, you could get on a phone and people would say 'I'll come help you out.' I felt very comfortable learning from people. People would tell their stories and everybody would listen.

"One other fun camping trip was at Black Rock just across the state line in Georgia. It was a primitive campsite, so there were no facilities. Everybody was squeamish about going to the bathroom. But it was peaceful. No cars, no trailers, and the night sky was dark. When we all stopped and listened all we could hear was nature. We could hear and see what God had made.

"On one mission trip we went to Washington, D.C., and held vacation Bible school for inner-city kids. We heard them tell us about shootings in the neighborhood, and they'd have to sleep below the level of the window sill. Being at the church was the safest they felt all day. We fed those children lunch, which may have been the best meal they ate that day. They knew what it meant to be safe in Christ.

"I've been a Sunday School teacher 21 or 22 years for children, youth, and young adults. The kids will teach you more than you learn sometimes doing your lesson. They'll say things that'll make you stop and think.

"The safest place I feel all week is right here with these people. If I've had a bad week, I look forward to getting up early and going to church. I feel better when it's over."

Interview: Lora Watson and Jean Mincey

July 5, 2011
by Nicole Jarosinski

Jean Mincey

Lora Watson

Upstairs of the church used to be full. People met in the central part, then would break up into classrooms for Sunday School. They had groups for Beginners, Primary, Intermediate, High School, Young People, and Adult.

Painter's daughter was Jean's Sunday School teacher. A classroom was where the pastor's office is now. It used to be the Hunter class, and Mrs. Hunter used to teach it.

College graduation used to be in the church because it was the largest building at the time. The college furnished half the money and land to build the church, and finally the church took over payments. College classes used to meet in the church for summer school. They met in the basement when Lora was in college. She had classes in the basement.

Both Jean and Lora were baptized in the creek, Lora before the baptistery pool was built and Jean after the pool was built but it was leaking. Both were baptized by Fred Forrester.

Lora remembers going to the old church when she was little. There was a "door on each side to go in." She only has a few memories of that building, and one of them was her first funeral. They had "outside toilets."

Lora: "The church was the center of all activities because we didn't have anything else. Not even a place to eat."

Jean: "Until Buck's Drug Store."

Lora remembers a chicken shack that may have gone in before Buck's.

At the new church building, the first minister Lora remembers is I.K. Stafford. He lived in a little house off to the side, which she thinks may have been the old parsonage. The church built a new parsonage when the Braswells came.

Lora: When Fred Forrester was pastor, women would quilt in the church and leave their [quilting rack] set up and leave it until they came back. Pastor Forrester had three little boys who would play around in the church. One day they were playing in the quilting room during meeting. A man walked in and found two boys had strung up the third on the quilting rack. The boy was hanging on the rack, standing on a chair, and the brothers were ready to kick the chair out from under him.

The church and college fussed over the road behind the church for years. It took a long time to settle the matter.

They decided (under Yelton) to buy land, sell the church, and build another. They found out they couldn't sell the church because if they didn't use it for church, it went back to the college. So the plan fell through.

The favorite pastor of both Lora and Jean is Braswell, then Hinson.

The church used to be full every Sunday. They'd have to bring in extra chairs for the service. Pastors would go around and visit people's homes. When Lora was young, the pastor used to come eat dinner with the family about twice a week. They usually drank wine with dinner so the pastor used to say they "Always had communion."

Lora: Johnny Long sat in front of Daddy in church. Daddy always sat on the back row and Johnny sat second to the back. Johnny would go to sleep nearly every Sunday. On one communion Sunday the usher passed the bread plate to Johnny, who pulled out a five dollar bill and put it on top of the bread. My daddy called him that afternoon and Johnny said "Well, at least you're the only one who saw it."

Some people left because they didn't like having a woman pastor, and some left after.

A big day for the church was always Decoration Day. People brought huge baskets of food. They'd spread it out on tablecloths on the ground. People came from all around, and the church had to cut it out because they couldn't feed all the people.

At Christmas all the kids would get presents. Lora remembers getting an orange, nuts, candy, and a ball when she was little. When she got older, she got things like clothes or shoes.

Gladys Parker, her sister Pearl Mashburn, and her neice Lucille used to do flowers all the time for the church. "They just took it upon themselves."

Lora had a real good Sunday School. The teacher would hand out leaflets with real pretty pictures on them like Moses in the bulrushes and there'd also be a memory verse. The kids would have to memorize the verses, do Bible drills, and memorize the order of books in the Bible.

The church had revivals every year. They'd be two weeks long. Lora would go to these, plus the one at Speedwell. Cullowhee's revivals were always more formal. At the revivals there'd be singing and more singing, preaching and more preaching, then somebody else would get up to preach. Some people would storm out. The older people would shout at Speedwell. One woman shouted every week at Cullowhee.

Lora: "I was little and never seen that before and I wondered what was wrong with her."

Lora came to Cullowhee Baptist because that's where her parents went when she was young. Later on her parents moved to Speedwell Baptist, but Lora stayed at Cullowhee.

Interview: Etheree Chancellor

June 27, 2011
by Nicole Jarosinski

N: I'm here with Etheree Chancellor who is going to share her experiences with Cullowhee Baptist Church. First question, how did you come to join Cullowhee Baptist Church?

E: We moved here in 1975, and my husband and I bought what was then Cullowhee Drugs. It was on campus, so we started attending this church.

N: What drew you in to CB?
E: Customers of the drug store inviting us.
N: And what made you decide to stay?
E: Because we lived here, and we worked here, and we liked it here, so we just stayed.

N: How have you been accepted by the church or by the people in the church? What makes it feel like home?
E: This church has become our family. We were transplants and had no family here. We were not really a part of the university and yet we were not locals. So we were just kinda hanging in the middle, and this church filled that space with a lot of love.

N: I was told you were the church secretary for 18 years.

E: That's right. We closed our drug store in 1986, and they were looking for a secretary here. The Personnel Committee asked me to work two weeks while they found a secretary. That two weeks lasted 18 years and two weeks.
N: What kind of things would you do?
E: I answered the phone; set up reservations for people to use the fellowship hall and sanctuary for weddings, funerals and family gatherings; set up meetings; sent out a lot of P.R. about anything that was going on in the church. At times I was responsible for seeing the Wednesday night meal was prepared, served, and the area cleaned for future use. I supervised the custodians. I was heavily involved with the youth, fundraisings, and anything people wanted me to do or help with, I pretty much did it. I was told that if a member came by or called and invited me to lunch, I should go. There wasn't much I didn't do.

N: What memories stand out to you about your time here in the church?
E: The first thing that pops to mind is when I came here there was no minister. Rev. Jack Hinson, pastor, had just resigned to go to the hospital as the first full-time chaplain there. Cathie Clayton and Kathy Lovedahl, who were deacons at the time, were responsible for getting a minister on each Sunday until we got a

minister. Most of those Sundays were filled by a minister from Mars Hill who was also an actor. Rev. Joseph Yelton was hired in the summer. I remember him coming in with these faded blue jeans and a Coca-Cola shirt on and saying, "So, tell me what's goin' on here." And I thought, well this guy's okay. He was a guy that had a great personality and loved people. He liked to visit as well as have members into their home for dinners. The senior adults enjoyed Joe's early morning visits. He took his young daughter Rosemary with him from time to time and then later his son Jake.

N: I have heard you did a lot for the cemetary. Tell us about that.
E: I developed a form and helped the cemetery committee send it to as many people as we could find names to send it, asking for donations and inviting them to the decoration. The form asked for their name, spouse, birthday, death date of their loved one, wedding date, their children, siblings, and the parents and grandchildren. The cemetery committee and I took those forms and with the help of a friend, put them all on the computer. If you will go to the Cullowhee Baptist webpage and click on cemetery, you should be able to pull this information. That has been a real asset to folks, especially those who are into genealogy.

N: What stands out to you about Cullowhee Baptist Church? When I say the words "Cullowhee Baptist" what pops out to you?
E: In my mind I see all these people that I've known from 1975 to present. I see faces—faces of members and WCU Baptist Student Union as well. I'm reminded of heartaches, I'm reminded of excitement, I'm reminded of good things and good times and bad times. It's just overflowing.

N: Do you have any stories you'd like to share?
E: We went on several mission trips. I've been to Honduras three times, but the church has been more times than that. Everything I have been involved in, if it needed a cook, I was it. Food and cleaning is my thing.
N: What was it that you did in Honduras?
E: With suitcases and duffle bags filled with food for Tom and Susan Canady and our own needs in hand, we drove to New Orleans Airport. The plane had left early...and left us. Fortunately for us, the airline found us free rooms in a motel at the end of the Mardi Gras parade. We had the best view as we watched from our motel windows at the parade turning around. Several of the men went into the streets and collected many pounds of necklaces that were being thrown out by those on the floats. The children in Honduras were excited to get them. We had taken small brown paper bags filled with candy, gum, and bouncy balls for each child who attended the LaMora church.

The first thing we did was to build an education building in LaMora. It was separate building from the church. One thing that was surprising to all of us, the windows had no screens or panes. It was just an open space in the walls. There were lots of children. Some of us went to the neighbors and took showers in their homes. Some had dirt floors. The missionary, Tom Canady and the men on the mission trip put a 50 gallon drum that had a spigot at the bottom for us to use for showers. That was quite different. One of the funniest things that happened on this trip was Pelham Thomas, who speaks some Spanish, said something to one of the teenage boys who was helping. The boy gave Pelham a strange look. Pelham asked Tom why was the boy giving him funny looks. After Pelham repeated what he had said to the boy, Tom broke up with laughter. Pelham had tried to tell the boy he was doing a good job but instead had told him he was a bad boy. Barbara Barlow, Galen Ernest, Pelham Thomas, Joe Yelton, and Paul and I were the ones from our church on this first of several trips. Johnny Buchanan and Larry Mace of neighboring churches went, and there were a couple from a former church of Joe's who went with us.

At Jerusalem Baptist the mission group, with the help of locals, started building a pastor's house a few feet from the church. We took our showers with a couple of baby iguanas. That was kind of eerie. I remember Lisa Dean, who is a Spanish teacher, went with us to teach Vacation Bible School and interact with the children in other ways. One day she came back from her walk with the kids and she said, "Children are children everywhere. They got in an argument about who was going to walk beside me and hold my hand."

One thing you know, it is not a rich country, but they went out of their way to feed us extremely well. I did all the cooking with the help of someone in our group, for three meals a day. And I'm not talking sandwiches because these guys had worked hard. We were not in air conditioning. It was hot, hot, hot. But each night before we were to leave a church and return home, they fixed us a big meal. That was really special because we knew they were giving us their best. Several locals would come by day to day and stand outside the fence and watch the workers who worked so hard to complete the walls of the block house before we left. The last night, those people came in—and others as they passed and saw the need—came into the fenced area. They formed a line making a human ramp from the ground to the top. They passed along the blocks up to the block layers and completed the walls very late that night. What a blessing it was to see those folks working together, and what a witness to see our guys welcome them in the group as they all worked together.

The last trip I went on was near the East coast of Honduras. On this trip we had Johnny Buchanan; Galen Ernest; Marie and Jim Searcy; Pelham Thomas; Corinne, Joe, Rosemary and Jake Yelton; Paul and myself. Marie helped me with the cooking as well as others pitching in. When the addition to the church was completed, it was used for Sunday School as well as a medical clinic during the week.

Our group attended church with the missionaries Tom and Susan on Sundays and Sunday nights and on Friday before we came home, we were taken into San Pedro Sula to shop and learn more of their culture.

Polly Burkett, Paul Chancellor, Mary Helderman, Keith Henry, Cordelia Meyer, Delores Nicholson, Dana Jones, Larry Mace, John Buchanan, Joe Yelton, Kirk Shufelt, Marie and Jim Searcy, Marie and Pelham Thomas were on other mission trips that worked on remodeling Third Baptist Church in San Pedro Sula.

N: Anything else you would like to share?
E: We had a Wednesday night meal, and I think Steve Baxley started this meal way back when I first started coming to this church. He prepared Wednesday night meals, and then his schedule changed so that he couldn't. Debra Martin, who was a sweet lady and a member of our church, donated her time also and cooked for a few years. So from time to time I did the Wednesday night meals, and then for years I was responsible for it. Tammy Gaetano also donated her time and prepared the meal. The two of us cooked together also. Oh, what fun! Once we were having so much fun, I forgot to put sugar in the cake. I poured it back into the mixing bowl and added sugar. No one was the wiser. Other women in the church—Dot Bell, Bonnie Hooper, Harriet Parker, and Jean Painter, and several other women—came on Wednesdays and cooked delicious home-cooked meals. Moquita Crawford told the funniest stories. And you'd know she wasn't really telling the truth all the time; you just knew it couldn't be true, but the way she told it was so funny you couldn't help but laugh about it. That was a fun time, cooking with all those ladies, or just being there and being a part of it was always a good time to have. And it was a good ministry. At 5 o'clock every Wednesday, someone took a plate of our home cooked food to the shut-ins of our church.

One of the things I remember is that on Sunday mornings when I first started coming here, was Lucille Painter, Gladys Parker, and her sister Pearl Mashburn were here every Sunday morning in the kitchen. They were fixin' beautiful bouquets of flowers from their gardens for the communion table. And then when we had Vacation Bible School little Lucille Painter, who was probably 4'10" and might have weighed 100 pounds soakin' wet, was in charge at that time of the cookies, the Moon Pies and the Kool-Aid for the school. She always wanted me to take her to the cheapest place. So I had to go to this grocery store to get two packs of Kool-Aid, and I'd have to go to a different grocery store to get cookies because they were on sale, and it just kept on. So finally about the third year I said, "Lucille, we're not doing this anymore. This gas is costing me more money than those cookies are costing. So you just make your list, and we're going to one place and we're gonna get it." So we did.

At Christmastime we had Hanging of the Greens. Poinsettias were bought in memory or honor of a loved one or friend by our members. Lucille loved to go with me to the greenhouse in Asheville. We would go over in the church van and fill it full. We never got the bows on the pots because she liked to make bows. She had owned a florist, and so she'd always make bows for those flowers and made them really pretty. The same way with Easter lilies. That was one of her big things. She was so short I had to help her in and out of the van because her legs couldn't reach the van step. These ladies were very faithful.

I remember Mike Vanzura, who was associate pastor, became full-time pastor after Joe Yelton. Mike was a soft-spoken man with a kind heart and was a good cook. I shall always be grateful for the coconut cream pies he made me for my birthday and at Christmas. Mike, as well as Joe, always made me feel as we were a team in ministry for the Lord.

In 1998 Mike and Terri Ducker, who worked with the children, developed this wonderful Christmas Eve Service which included 40 men and women representing Jesus' ancestors. Each ancestor, with candle in hand, walked down the aisle and placed their candle on the communion table and read their name and how they were related to Jesus.

It made such an impression on me. I approached Mike with the idea of going on a bigger scale with this presentation and invite enough people to have every one of Jesus' ancestors walk down the isle in full costume. The idea kept growing and including to extend the program to end as 13-year-old Jesus.

We approached Amy Garza, who is a member of our church and an author, to write a play including all the ancestors. And so it was, *The Trail of Light* was born. Knowing there wasn't enough in our congregation to carry this out, we decided to invite other denominations to join us—and they did. Methodist, Presbyterian, Baptists, Catholics, non-denominational,Unitarians, and atheists participated.

After Amy wrote the play, the small committee met and approved the script, including dancers for King David, and the first production of *The Trail of Light* was held on a cold, cold December night beside the church. I daresay we are the only Baptist church in Jackson County or maybe Western North Carolina that has allowed dancing in the church—but as one of our deacons who approved the script said, "It's Biblical. They danced for King David and he certainly was one of Jesus' ancestors." The Jackson County Recreation Department brought a couple of portable seating stands for the audience. We even had a real mule for "Mary" to ride. Rev. Jack Hinson, a former pastor, was the narrator and did an outstanding job. Eventually we had characters from 31 different churches to participate.

The second year, and those that followed the next eight years, were held in Cullowhee Baptist because of the cold weather. It was a tight fit and a successful ministry. Each year we added more new costumes and props as well as additions to the drama itself. The last four years, the drama was extended to include Jesus as a man and was called *Mary Did You Know?* The last year, in 2008, a busload of tourists came through our beautiful mountains and attended the drama. It ended on a positive note.

I can tell you a little bit about the Vickerys. It was a big transition for me to make when Vanzura left and when the Vickerys came. One thing is because the Vickerys brought in the use of computers and email more. Sometimes it's hard to teach an old horse new tricks. So I felt like I was the old horse trying to learn a new trick. We welcomed them, and I thought it was sorta neat that we had a man and a woman serving as pastor. Now, Jack Hinson's wife was the director of the music at one time as was Joe Yelton's wife, so it was not uncommon for pastor and wife to work together, but it was uncommon to have them work together as pastors. But it wasn't surprising to me because we had a woman preacher living in our tenant house on our farm and I heard her preach. But it was a different thing for this church and for this area for that to happen. I'm glad I was here to be a part of that transition. I only worked as secretary a couple of years with the Vickerys before I retired.

Well, I have been thinking of the question "What is the most memorable time while secretary or while a member?" It was the completion of a much long-awaited newly renovated kitchen and fellowship hall. One Wednesday I was working in the kitchen preparing for the Wednesday evening meal, and I saw a black snake go behind the refrigerator. I immediately called one of the fix-it-and-fix-it-now members, Pete Lovedahl. Pete was one of the men in the congregation I could always count on when needed. Pete came down and I explained the snake had come out of the old heat vent and gone under the refrigerator and then behind a cabinet. I need a long skinny something to go behind there, he said, so I ran upstairs into my office and grabbed a yard stick. As I handed him the yard stick, I jumped up into a chair.

Now when I poke back here and he comes out, you head him off.

Are you kidding me? I asked.

He then looked at me and spoke in a louder voice, What are you a doing up there in that chair?

Getting out of the way of the snake! I answered.

You can't kill no snake standing in that chair! he said still in a louder voice.

I know, I said in my louder voice. That's why I called you.

He killed the snake, and we both had a good laugh. That wasn't the first nor the last time we had a snake in the kitchen or in the hallway joining the kitchen. The remodeling took care of lots of things, including snake intrusion. When we had the kitchen dedication, I was presented the vent from which the snake came.

I am grateful that Reverends Mike Vanzura and Wanda Kidd were with my family in Asheville when Mom moved to Heaven. I shall always be grateful also for Keith Henry, who accompanied Mike the 18-plus hours round-trip to comfort my family and give Mom her last rites.

It was beyond the call of duty for my friends Pam Martin and Kathy Lovedahl to accompany the Reverends Tonya and Jeffrey Vickery all the way to South Alabama to comfort my family in another time of grief—the funeral of my beloved husband of 44-plus years and best friend, Paul.

John and Cathie Clayton

Onifer and Meagan Wilmoth

Interview: James Dooley

July 12, 2011
by Nicole Jarosinski

N: I'm here with James Dooley, who is going to share his memories of Cullowhee Baptist Church. You said you were a choir director for about two years. Which years were they?
J: 1996–1998. It may not have been a full two years, but it was in that time period. I was more or less an interim time to bridge the gap between the one who'd been here before and the one who came after.

N: What was a typical week like for you as the director?
J: Being only part-time, my responsibilities were simply to prepare the choir at a practice during the week and direct the choir and the music in the church service on Sunday morning. So that was not a task requiring lots of hours. Because I had a tremendous amount of experience in the past, it didn't require that I do an inordinate amount of preparation.

N: Did I hear you were involved with music for a long time as part of your job?
J: I came here in 1969 as head of the department of music at the university and served in that capacity for a number of years before moving into the administrative side of the university.

N: Do you have any stories you'd like to share about the choir while you were the director?
J: First of all, I would say the church has enjoyed and benefited from being on the campus. There was an influence from the university in its early days from people who were trained for music careers because the university itself was founded with a very strong emphasis on the arts, more so than most institutions of that period, bearing in mind that many of the institutions, especially in rural areas of North Carolina, would not have access to trained musicians. If you were to go out and pick a church at random in the rural area of any state, you would find they might have more difficulty attracting leadership and keyboard players or organ players simply because if you're out in the rural area, the likelihood that you're gonna run up against a really sophisticated musician, it's not very great. Because the university was here and began with a very heavy emphasis on the arts, the church benefited from that. The students also were attracted to singing in the choir because that was a very good outlet for them. If you look at the history of the church and take into account some of the activities and the numbers of people who were involved in those activities, you'll notice right away that before World

War Two, back in the 30s and 40s, the choir was large, and one of the reasons was the students. There was for a time a college-age student choir in the church. So this church has benefited from being on the campus in many different ways, and music has been one of them.

N: Yeah. Mr. Wood was saying we had the best choir than everywhere around for that same reason. We had all the professionals. And in other churches if you just wanted to go up and sit in with the choir for the day you could. You just joined the choir.

J: Right. Because of the university influence, we did not have the kind of music that you would find in other churches. Are you familiar with the gospel quartet music?

N: Quartet? No.

J: Quartets, male quartets typically, that would sing more lively music (snaps fingers), and there are churches in this area, near here, that have had that kind of music program. Ours is a little more sedate, and it's a little more grounded in the history of church music than those that follow the more popular sounds. Do you know enough about music and church music to know what I'm talking about?

N: Not really, no.

J: Okay. Well, early in the 20th century, we had the development of Sunday School songs and more popular-sounding songs with rhythms that were a little catchier, not as grounded in tradition. Traveling quartets would usually have a piano player who could really play ragtime piano, and occasionally they had instruments with them—a string bass player, and guitar players in some cases. That would have been a style of music attractive to a lot of people, a very popular-sounding music. The more historic-based churches and music programs would be conducive to worship, but not have the pep. Make sense?

N: Yeah. Sometimes when I'm in church and I have the hymnal I'll start looking at the dates. Many writers seemed to live about 1870 to 1930, give or take.

J: Are you talking about the music or just in general?

N: Those are the dates of the songwriters. They're the lifespans and somewhere in there that song was written. Sometimes when I'm singing the songs, I get Carrie Nation in my head singing "Onward Christian Soldiers" as she goes to crack some whiskey barrels. I see sometimes a connection with the history in the songs. And then there's definitely a feel in some of the hymns about what's a little bit newer versus what's older.

J: Yeah. Musical styles have taken many different paths. If you get into a really thoroughgoing study, you'll find many streams that will take you way off from the earliest sedate music that you would picture a line of monks singing. The popular or recreational music, folk music particularly, became a very important influence on church music through the centuries. In the United States, music was extremely important from the very beginning of the forming and settlement of the country. The people who came to settle America usually came from churches that had very strong commitment programs. They were really enthusiastic about their religion. So you find a great deal of that going in different directions. Are you familiar at all with shape-note singing? Have you heard anything about the Mi Fa Sol La Singers? You'll find a very strong element of shape-note singing in this area because rural churches, being way out from civilization, became their own teachers. They were self-taught. You're familiar with Do Re Mi Fa Sol La Ti Do, if nothing else from *The Sound of Music*. That's a method of learning to read music, the notes of the scale. You gain a mental connection when you sing that scale. You hear all of that and you remember it, and it's a terrific way to teach people to read music. And then they got the idea that if we give the note heads a different shape, it'll be even easier. That's where shape notes came from, if you've heard the term before. It would be a shock to people who had never been exposed to it. I formed a community chorus here back in 1970, and occasionally I had them sing a shape-note tune. Most of them had heard of it, that is to say the technique, but hadn't really learned it and practiced it. But it is a very, very important element in western music, in all of Western Europe and especially the United States, because the musicians early on learned to read music with the syllables. That has become one of the historic streams in this area that has continued. There is one place fairly close to Asheville that has been having annual singings for generations. Not years but generations. They sing the repertoire of shape-note singers. They have their own book.

N: So it sounds totally different?

J: They know what the syllables are, and they can always remember how Do and Sol sound in relation one to the other.

N: When they sing a song do they sing just the syllables?

J: The shape-note singers have gone a step farther because they don't sing only the syllables because of where it falls in the scale, but they use another help which is the shape of the head instead of just the oval.

N: Ok, so looking at it on a page, they have a different symbolary?

J: You've seen this before?

N: No, I'm trying to figure it out.

J: I should have brought one for you to see. Note heads are triangles, ovals, squares, and diamonds. And they know how the diamond sounds in relation to the oval, and when they see the diamond, they note what pitch because it sounds this way compared to Do. And that's what Maria was doing in *The Sound of Music*. She was teaching the children to learn the sound. If you can remember how Re sounds in relation to Do, you can read anything. You don't have to do it just abstractly by looking at where the note is on the staff. A scale is an abstract concept. And early on in history, people learned how to make it concrete by writing it down, by drawing it on lines. In this area we have what we call traditional style, which is pretty straightforward and dignified in most cases, and as someone would say, boring. And we have also the shape-note singers, who sing many of the same hymns, but it's a different set and it's a different style, it's a different culture. Then you have the gospel singers, the quartets, and they have an entirely different style too. This church's style is pretty close to the traditional, where you find it in the First Church of whatever—Methodist, Lutheran—in any town.

N: Sometimes when we're singing, I can't help but think of this British comedian who tells a joke about the Church of England and how very formal they are. He talks about them singing and they're not even joyful. Very dull singing.
J: And that is the motivating attitude and thinking that has promoted and generated the various styles of singing that we hear in church. It's fair to say that if you fall into a rut and don't try to find and experience the emotion of traditional music, it can be dull as dirt. You have to seek it. You have to go after it. You have to uncover it. And that's the job of the choir director, to get people to understand that what they're singing is not just a tradition, but it has meaning, it has real energy in it. A lot of people can't do that, or they don't want to because they're attracted to another style.

N: It seems like the joy and the emotion really comes out in the choir's anthem or in the prelude from the organ and piano.
J: The anthem is good, but that has become a generic term. It's the choir's turn where we're going to sing for you something that's meaningful for us and we hope that you will catch that too. That's the choir's aim, that's their goal. The choirs first goal is to energize themselves and secondly to do that for the congregation. Our choir director here understands that. He understands, too, that you can do it a lot of different ways, and he's chosen the traditional way, which is challenging but also very rewarding. And he does a good job of it.

N: Connor Davis' solo last week, that was pretty moving. I got chills.
J: And that's very conservative music, very conservative. It's not snappy, and yet it did something for you, didn't it? And it didn't hurt that Connor is a very, very sensitive musician to be as young as he is. He plays well in the first place. When you play an instrument, technique is a very important factor. And you have to have a good instrument. There has to be some soul, and he has that. He can hear it, and he can produce it.

N: Going back to the students from Western in the choir, did they used to get school credit?
J: I think there was a time where that happened. I can't say with certainty. When an institution is that close, interwoven as it was here, it's quite possible, especially in the early days when it was so remote. Even Sylva was like a foreign country. When you're in a remote area like this was, and there wasn't a lot for young people to get involved in, this was a pretty good deal. Think of it in terms not just of what they could do for this church in providing music for the service, but what the church did for them. It's a very rewarding kind of thing.

N: Do you have any other stories you'd like to share about the choir?
J: One thing I think is important, we have had for the last 15 years or so: young people have been singing with the choir, and it has become all girls. The idea of bringing them in to sing with the

adults is something that Steve has done, which has been a really positive move. It has bolstered the choir, it has given these young ladies tremendous opportunity to interact and generate something with adults, in league with adults. I think that's an awfully intelligent thing to do, but it's also something that has made a difference. It's rejuvenated the adults in the choir. They respond to it very positively. When you meet with Steve, ask him what motivated him to do that other than to get some more sopranos. Because that has been a very successful merging of abilities and generations.

N: I have some general questions. First, what would you like to say to future members?
J: I just have a fairly simple message, and that is if you want a church that has warm relations among its members, has excellent, well-educated, knowledgeable, talented leadership, a church that maintains and perpetuates the best of traditional worship practices, and also has a membership that is warm, easy to get to know, and friendly, this is a good place to be.

N: How did you first come to join Cullowhee Baptist?
J: My wife and I both grew up in a church not unlike this. We weren't on a college campus, but there were many characteristics of this church that were very close to what we were accustomed to. Because of the university, I think this has a dignified and very serious as well as happy and jovial personality. We liked the idea of going to church with people we knew we were going to be associating with professionally and socially. It fit our needs.

N: What do you look forward to every year?
J: I enjoy the buildup to the Christmas season, and I feel good about the way our ministers handle that. We use the church calendar, which is not common in Baptist churches. But what is rewarding is we have periods like Advent and the buildup for Christmas. It's done not in a commercial way but in a thoughtful way. The same thing is true with Lent, and most Baptist churches don't really talk about Lent. It's a very rewarding experience to observe those periods in which we can focus on aspects of our own personal lives and our relationship to others.

N: What was a significant moment for you as a member here in the church?
J: One of the good things about this church is that all the surprises are good surprises. And they tend not to be connected with the health and vigor of the church. So you don't expect something really catastrophic happening. There's been a couple of times, admittedly where I was a little concerned in the past about where we were heading. I think all of us who do value church membership and go to church regularly are concerned that there is a diminution in general. We're not the only congregation that has experienced the loss of total membership. It's hard for any of us to try to look out for the future and figure out where we're going to be.

N: Thank you very much for your time.
J: I enjoyed talking with you.

Interview: Dianne Yount

July 20, 2011
by Nicole Jarosinski

N: First things first, how did you come to join Cullowhee Baptist?
D: We lived in Cullowhee two different times. We were here from 1970 – 1973 while my husband was in school at Western, and we would have stayed at that time but he could not find a job. So we left and after two years he was able to come back. We came back to Cullowhee in 1975, he as teacher and coach at Camp Laboratory School, which included Cullowhee High School, and we wanted to go to the church in our community. When we moved back our son was seven, and we wanted him to grow up in our community church.

N: How do you feel you have been accepted by Cullowhee Baptist?
D: I feel we have been accepted very well. It feels like home. We were welcomed very warmly by the congregation, by the pastor. When we did join, I think I remember the pastor saying, "It's about time," so we felt like we were already members, and I think some people felt like we already were before we actually joined.

N: What do you look forward to in the church?

D: We don't have Wednesday night services during the summer, and it really is exciting when we first start back, and it usually coincides with the beginning of school. That's one thing I sort of miss about teaching, that excitement at the beginning of the school year. And it's the same thing here. I just sort of feel that excitement beginning with our Wednesday night meal and our Bible study. It really feels good to get back to that and get back into the routine. I also really enjoy Sunday morning Bible study and it's always interesting to try to bring in other people's ideas and what they see in the scripture for the lesson.

N: How have you been affected by Cullowhee Baptist? How has it impacted your life?
D: It makes me want to read the scripture in a way that it becomes more personal to me and that I understand it better so that it changes me as a person. It changes the way I look at life, the way I view different situations and circumstances and people.

N: What do you remember about

previous pastors?
D: Each one had unique personalities, and most of them have had in their own way really interesting senses of humor. I love humor, and most of them have managed to include humor in many different ways in Bible studies and sermons. Each one is different, as it should be. Each person is different. So it just makes sense that each pastor would bring his or her personality to the church.

N: What was a significant moment for you being here?
D: Probably when Tonya and Jeffrey came. I was on the deacon board at the time and just everything we went through with the Association not accepting that and not willing to let us make our own decisions about who should be pastor of our church. It was a real growing experience for us, and we had to decide as a church that we wanted to take a stand for what we believed in. It might not have been the popular thing to do and we did lose some members, but we just felt like that's what we should do. We really believed it was the right thing to do. So that was a real growing experience.

N: What was your role as all that was progressing?
D: Just as a member, to show support for the decisions that were made, that the church made as a whole, because the church makes the decisions. One or two people can't make the decisions even though they might want to. We were sort of on the fence for a while. We remained Southern Baptist while we were also Cooperative Baptist Fellowship. We did that for some time, but then there came a time when we realized it was time to become Cooperative Baptist Fellowship. So we did. I didn't take a major role in it. I was just a member of the church and supported that.

N: They had your vote.
D: Yes that's right. That's right. (Laughs)

N: What was your happiest moment in the church?
D: Well, probably my happiest moment would have to be when our son was baptized because obviously it was not something he did just because his friends were doing it or somebody asked him to do it or somebody told him he should do it. It was a decision that he made on his own, and at the age of 16 that's a difficult time to make decisions like that. But he made that decision and he was baptized. That would probably have to be my happiest moment. And then when he and his wife wanted to get married here. That was a happy time, too.

N: Do you have any stories you would like to share?
D: One thing that we have done for the

past couple years that was a lot of fun but also raised money was a cake auction. We have it on a Sunday after church in winter and people bring desserts. That's a lot of fun to participate in that way. I can remember when we had the last one early this year, at least one child got involved in the bidding. He was sitting with his father so his father would say it was okay. We were raising money for the line item in our budget that covers the Wednesday night meals because college students eat free and anybody who can't pay is welcome to come. People who can pay do, but college students eat free and there are some meals that are carried out to people in the community who can't come. We usually need money for that line item, and that was a lot of fun. And working together to accomplish things, like the renovation of the fellowship hall and the air conditioning. That involved people committing to work together and give over a period of time to help pay for that. It's just such a sense of working together, cooperating, and camaraderie.

N: Would you say this church does that for most things? Is there a real culture of cooperation?
D: I think so. Of course not everybody is going to be gung-ho about everything, but I think there is a real effort to cooperate and accomplish things that we feel need to be accomplished.

N: Is there anything else you would like to add?
D: I think Cullowhee Baptist has always been mission-minded, and it's been interesting to see over the years how that's played out in the congregation. Now we talk about missional churches and that is, rather than giving money to send somewhere, which we do too, but really getting involved in things that need to be done in our community as well as other places. We've had a partnership, as a CBF church, we have groups go out to Helena, Arkansas. Phillips County is identified as one of the poorest counties in the country. And CBF has been working on a 20-year program. Over 20 years they want to work with people in these communities and do what they can. So churches all over the country send groups to these different areas to work and do what needs to be done. We've also had people go to Ukraine and work over there. We've had college students go to Pine Ridge Indian Reservation in South Dakota. They've gone to lots of different places. But just to see the involvement of people going and helping people, but doing a lot of that here too. Especially getting youth involved.

N: What would you like to say to future members? Do you have a message you'd like to give?
D: It would have to be to stand up for what you believe is right. To know what is right according to the Bible and to be willing to stand up for that even if it means taking an unpopular stance. To know the Bible, to study the Bible, and try to live according to the Bible. And by the same token, realize that other people might not believe exactly the way you do, but if they're living the way they think the Bible says they should live, then we have to allow a place for that grace. And of course that's our motto: a place of grace and peace.

Interview: Wanda Kidd

July 7, 2011
by Nicole Jarosinski

N: My first question is why did you choose Cullowhee Baptist? What drew you in about this place?
W: I was an undergrad here, so I attended church as a student. What drew me at that point was a real sense that Cullowhee was a place. It was not just a university. It had an identity and neighborhoods. There was a real strong sense of the town and the gown, and lots of professors in the 70s came to worship here and that was a lovely thing to see them in the classroom and to see them as people of faith as well. I was drawn to it because of the people. Gladys Parker was one; she welcomed and made every young adult feel like she personally was delighted that you had walked through this door. I remember that summer vividly, people lining up to come and welcome me. I had left Jackson County to live in South Carolina for 10 years and came back to do an internship at the BSU for two years. They were looking for a youth minister at Cullowhee Baptist, so I applied. Since I was through with seminary then, I came on as the Youth and Children's Minister. The church was booming at that point. The sanctuary was full. I was the chaplain to the boys' basketball team at the high school, and I travelled with them everywhere. Many of the basketball players came to the youth group. I worked here for two years, and it was a great time.

N: Can you tell me about what Richard did here?
W: This campus ministry has grown from nothing to 20 people. So it's the fastest growing one nationally. And that was all because of Richard.

N: Do you have any stories about youth trips?
W: I have one that always comes to mind. I had already left the church but had committed to take the youth on a beach trip. This is before cell phones. We had a couple of vans following another vehicle. We were riding down I-26 toward Myrtle Beach, and the engine blew in my van. So we pulled off the road and another van pulled up behind us. A hippie-looking woman with two small children got out and she said, "I saw your engine blow. Would you like to go to my house and make some phone calls?" There were two other adults with us and a few students. So she drove us to her house and she had all these games and things at her house. They were really old hippies. They had lived in a bus, and that bus

was still in the yard. She let me go into her house and make calls, but it was Father's Day, June 19, so nobody was home. I knew people in that part of the state but nobody was home. I called back up here and they said, "Oh, you'll figure it out." So I just started calling random churches and about the eighth call—to Boiling Springs—and I said, "Hello, I'm Wanda Kidd. I'm on a youth beach trip and we're here in Spartanburg and the engine blew and we can't fix it for days." This would not happen at all now, not on any level. None of this story would compute to anybody. Nobody would get in a car with a stranger, you would call, and every parent would come and pick their child up individually. So the pastor answered and he said, "Are you the Wanda Kidd that was in seminary with me in 1983?" And I said, "I am a Wanda Kidd that was in seminary." He said, "Wait just a minute. My van committee is here meeting at the church right now. So he went and presented and they voted that we could borrow their van for the week. I'm supposed to pick it up in the parking lot at Westgate Mall. Somebody drives me over there and I get in and they give me this lecture about blah blah blah. My favorite line was when the man said, "I only ask one thing of ya. Do not besmirch the name on the side of this van." (Laughs) I said, "I'll do my best." Now the other people on the trip have left, they don't know where we are. We had no cell phones. I had the key to get into the house at Myrtle Beach so it was just a nightmare. But anyway we had a great time and we did not besmirch the name on the side of that van.

One time we were supposed to go camping for spring-break weekend. We were going to Cade's Cove, and I was up all night off and on because there were reports that it was snowing in Cade's Cove. I came to church early to tell the parents that we weren't gonna go, but by the time I got here six kids were here with their stuff and their parents had dropped them off and gone...left me with them. So we took a pencil and drew a two hour radius around here and looked for state parks. There was a state park in Paris Mountain, South Carolina, so we went camping there. And a windstorm came through and blew over a tree that crushed a RV next to us. But we were okay by the grace of God.

We went to the state championships for the basketball team that year. That was great fun. We did a lot of Bible studies on David and Goliath cuz it was such a tiny little school. In '86 when VHS was just coming out, I bought a copy of *Footloose* and we used it as a Bible study on secret keeping. It was a good time for the youth; they traveled a little bit, they did a musical. There were 30-35 kids in that group. That's a good youth group even now for any size church. There's always this floating youth group that kids will invite their friends to and you don't have to belong to the church. This was the community youth group to come to for that few years. We talk often about having a reunion with that group of kids. It's been 20-some years now. They're all grown, but none of them are in this church. Some are going to the Summit. Several have gone into the ministry out of that youth group.

Have you heard about Annie Hoyle? She gave every penny she had and she invested her whole life in this church. The youth started the Valentine

Banquet and it continued after I left. It became a church-wide thing. But we started it as the youth inviting senior adults to the Valentine Banquet and doing all the serving. I just always remember that because Annie, oh she hated me. The first Valentine Banquet, that Sunday after church I said, "Ms. Annie, are you coming to lunch?" "No, I did not get an invitation." So I said, "I'm really sorry. I'm pretty sure I sent you one." "No, you did not." So the next year I said to her, "So, Ms. Annie, are you coming to the Valentine Banquet?" "No, I did not get an invitation." I said, "Ms. Annie that's not true. I sent yours registered mail so you would not say that to me in public again." She had to sign for it. But she came that year. Later I was working with the Methodist church. She had a massive heart attack and drove herself to the hospital. I was visiting somebody else at the hospital, and Annie was in the next room. I just stood in that hall and argued with myself and argued. So I knocked on the door and said, "Ms. Annie, it's Wanda Kidd." And she said, "Please come in." I went in and she just apologized for all the things she had ever said and done to me and how she felt really badly that she had done that. We had this moment of grace and forgiveness, and she died a week later. It was just a really good moment for both of us. I would have missed the blessing had I not gone in there. Ms. Annie was a presence for 50 years in this church. She started the BSU. They started meeting in the basement at Cullowhee Baptist before that. She had lots of high lofty ambitions and got things done and accomplished some really good things.

N: Is there anything you would like to say to future members?

W: What I want to say to us today so that we would hopefully have members in the future is to create a space and respect for open discourse and ministry that's based in scripture. My hope for the future is that people feel like their voice is heard and respected and then acted upon. "We've heard your voice," and then ask, "What are we gonna do about that? Why would we do that and then how would we do that?"

Harrill and Phoebe Hooper and Cindy

Mary Lou and Amy Millwood, 1992

Interview: Charles and Pam Hill

Date: June 28, 2011

by Nicole Jarosinski

N: I'm speaking with Mr. and Mrs. Hill, who are going to share their experiences from Cullowhee Baptist Church. First, how did you come to join Cullowhee Baptist Church?

P: We moved into this house in August 1997. The previous owner was Joe Yelton, a former pastor of Cullowhee Baptist, and as we came to inspect the house before closing, he was still here moving things out. We asked him what a good Baptist church nearby would be, knowing he would probably mention his church, which he did. Since it was the closest Baptist church, we were gonna start visiting at Cullowhee Baptist and maybe branch out and see some others. We never left. When we first walked in we met Thelma Dills at the front door and asked her if there was a couples' class for Sunday school. She said, "I didn't know of any but you can come into my class," which was the women's class. The men's class was outside in the cemetery because it was Decoration Day, so we both went to the King's Daughters class, the women's class. That was sort of funny. A few minutes later the preacher's wife came up to

tell us there was a couples class down in the basement. So we were only in the ladies' class for a few minutes then we went downstairs.

N: What drew you in? What made you decide to stay at Cullowhee Baptist?
P: First of all, the Sunday school class. It was just a good group of people and we had a good discussion that day. Then, in church service, Mike Vanzura, the pastor, mentioned the priesthood of believers, which is something we very much believe in. Since there are a lot of different kinds of Baptist churches we thought, well, this sounded pretty good. We came back several times and joined probably about a month later. Maybe two months. We met a lot of good people we liked. And people remembered our names when we came back the second Sunday. That always impresses people. Gladys Parker was one of them who remembered our names. She was good about finding new people and talking to them. We've always been at a much bigger church before, so this was a big change for us. And we didn't know anybody in Cullowhee or anybody in Western North Carolina when we moved here. It was nice to meet people who were very kind.

N: How have you been accepted by the church? What let you know that you were part of the family now?
P: Well Etheree Chancellor, who was the secretary then, called me out the week we joined and said, "Pam, we need some help with the bazaar the church is doing and can you be available?" So she got me involved right from the beginning. We started meeting people and working different things. Etheree was really good about getting people involved. She would just pick up the phone and call and say, "I need you. Come on over." So that's how we sorta got into things.

N: You know you're in it when Etheree calls you.
P: Right. Right. She just called as a matter of fact.
C: There have been times we wished we weren't quite as involved, but once you get involved, it's hard not to be. And I guess that's certainly better than not being involved at all.

N: What is one thing that sticks out in your mind about your time in Cullowhee Baptist Church? One event or moment?
C: I guess the moment that hits home the strongest to me was the time that we went with church members to a Tuckaseigee Baptist Association meeting. Wilma Cosper, one of our members, was on a committee there, and we knew the topic of that committee was our church and the calling of a woman pastor. We also knew they were trying to have a secret meeting without Wilma knowing about it. Deacons went to this meeting and other members came along too, but they wouldn't let us inside the meeting. So, we sat out in the cold and waited for

Wilma Cosper

Wilma to go inside. That group was a big cross section of the church, some of which probably did not really want to call a woman pastor, but they didn't want to see the church dissed for making the decision, which in Baptist tradition is the church's decision. That was a strong statement.

N: What do you do with people in the church?
C: Pelham Thomas, an 89-year-old member, he runs the group that build ramps. the last time there were only three of us that went, but sometimes we'll have 10 of us there. If it's a big ramp project and we know it's gonna take a lot of help, he usually puts a little pressure on people. That's a good experience, you know, helping out someone.
P: We go to the softball games.
C: We're known as the chief fans.
P: We're the cheerleaders.
C: We told 'em we're not gonna go out on the field and play softball anymore.

N: What do you look forward to every year? Any kind of events that go on? Or special days?
C: Well this year we're looking forward to the 190th anniversary and we've been through the 180th before. At 200 years they're gonna dig up the time capsule, so we do hope to be here next time.

P: They had just finished the 175th when we got here. They had painted the sanctuary, and done a lot of things like that.

C: The first meeting we went to when we got here, the discussion was of the plans to renovate. They'd already rejected a plan to build a new addition on the side, which Joe Yelton had been involved with, and which may or may not have been one of the reasons that he left. Anyway, the plan they had that night was gonna be either $1.1 or $1.3 million. Now this was 15 years ago, but even in today's standard that's a pretty big debt hanging on 'em. One of the strong members of the church was Stedman Mitchell. Stedman doesn't come every Sunday now, he's 95 and it's a little tough for him, but he still gets out. Stedman believed we didn't' need to do anything we can't pay for, to get the money up first. Well we all knew we couldn't save up $1.3 million, so renovations just sorta went by the wayside. About eight or ten years later, we got started on it again and we finally narrowed down what we wanted to do the most. Well, in between there we did do some renovation. We did some of what we call core, new electrical, things like that. But they're the things you don't see. Everyone was upset about that because we spent about $300,000 and couldn't see it. So the next time we said, "It's gotta be something we see." We did the fellowship hall, and it's been nothing but positive. That got us motivated to do more. We have a lot of members who were against air conditioning because they grew up here and they thought you didn't need to have air conditioning. I finally got one or two to admit they didn't come as much in the summer because it was hot. So we did finally move on air conditioning. In another year or two when that's over with we'll find something else we want done.

N: Etheree was telling me there's a culture in the church of not wanting to owe money. So they always pay things off early.

C: Right. The fellowship hall, the downstairs, we originally planned on five years, but we paid it off in less than two. So that's pretty great. And we'll have this air conditioning paid off probably within a year.

N: Do you have any stories about any of the pastors since you've been here?

C: Before we actually called the Vickerys, we went down to the community in South Carolina where they had preached. Jeffery preached that Sunday, then we went out to lunch with them. Of course all this was supposed to be a secret. There's a committee of six or eight people and no one knows that you're there to see these pastors when they're still working at that church. A couple on the committee had been a little shocked over the possibility of calling co-pastors. Anyway, Dr. Vosecky was along on the trip. He was a little more conservative, and he seemed to like them. He turned to Tonya and said something about, "It might be good if Jeffrey could come as the chief pastor and you be the associate." And before she could even respond, Jeffrey said, "That won't happen. This is a team, we're a team, and we will both come as your pastors." And first of all, the fact that he stood up so fast himself, and then she did also, and we thought, that's a good team. It worked well. I'm' sure that we had a few people leave the church, maybe not right away but over time, because they didn't like having a woman pastor, but not many. It was pretty well accepted. And almost every church in town that's at least a little bit moderate thinks we've made one devil of a good choice.

N: What was a significant moment for you as a member?

P: Well, Charles talked about going with the deacons over to the Association meeting. I went to a meeting after that and we knew that the Tuckaseigee Baptist Association really wanted to vote Cullowhee Baptist out of the Association just so they wouldn't have a woman pastor in a church. They refused to put Tonya's picture up on the wall of pastors that were currently serving in the county. We had gone that evening for an open meeting, but I knew it would not be a happy time. I wouldn't be able to speak that night because only the pastors were going to be speaking, but I had just finished reading *The Tall Woman* by Wilma Dykeman, which is a mountain story. Since Tonya's very tall, I decided to make my statement by bringing the book with me. I carried it so that the title showed and sat with it on my lap. That was a way to make a statement. Anyway, very soon after they opened the meeting, one of the pastors stood up and wanted a closed meeting, which they had never had before. They voted for a closed meeting, and all the people that were not pastors were asked to leave. We walked out, and of course I held the book so they could see it going out also. But Charles Dean, who was pastor of East Sylva, walked out with us. Members of the press from *Sylva Herald* were waiting outside, and there were other members standing around wondering what was gonna happen in the meeting. We asked Charles why he had walked out and he said, "I haven't been in a closed meeting in my life and I refuse to participate." Now East Sylva did back us although they're not as moderate as we are. I really liked that he walked out, you know, and made a statement. And later on when we decided to voluntarily get out of the Association instead of going through all of that stuff they were doing, East Sylva and First Baptist in Sylva left also.

C: I think there were five churches including ourselves that left.

P: But it was an uneasy time. We had a meeting at our church soon thereafter and Jeffrey was saying we need to make a decision instead of going on and on and on with this because it's really dragging us down. Tonya and Jeffrey could not get their programs started with all this other stuff going on. One member who worked for the radio station here in town said, "You know I've been in public relations, and your public relations would be a lot better if you didn't have all this going on. You could go on and start your programs and start advertising what's good," which made a whole lot of sense. So we decided to get out of the Association. And we did. It was just sort of a messy time.

N: The church is still out of the Association right?

P: Right. We're still out.

C: It hit us the other day that this is not over. We were at a softball game 10 years from this time, and they were gonna open the game up and the umpire asked if there was a preacher there to give a prayer.

P: The two teams had gotten together.

This wasn't the audience or anything.
C: They asked for a preacher to give a prayer, and Tonya was the only preacher there. She said "I'm a preacher." The umpire just didn't recognize her at all and went on to look for another preacher or a man. Anything. One of our members who was on the team said, "Tonya can handle that." And then she stepped forward and prayed. All the people, even on the other team and not involved in our church, commented about that, and they were sad it had happened. It just brings home that those things take a long time to change.
P: Well, there was something that had happened at a recent wedding at our church. The couple had decided on a Baptist preacher from another church and were going to have the wedding at our church.
C: He was the pastor of the groom's family.
P: The week of the wedding he found out that Tonya was also involved in the ceremony and he said he wouldn't do the wedding at our church with Tonya involved. Tonya went to the couple and said, "I am not gonna mess up your wedding day, and I'll step aside if that's what you want." So even in our own church the pastor coming in said he wouldn't work with her. That was sad because this was supposed to be a happy day.
C: He was willing to ruin their day over this thing he wanted.
P: But this still goes on.

N: What was your happiest moment as part of the church?
C: Probably paying off the note for the renovation downstairs. Everyone enjoyed that.
P: Since he's on the finance committee.
C: It was just a sense of accomplishment. First of all, it was done very well. And second, we got it paid off. We did have a lot of the money earned beforehand. We had saved for years to get to the point where we could start that. And we done the same thing with air conditioning. And as soon as we figure out our next plan, hopefully by the time we pay off the air conditioning, we'll probably start a fund drive for something else.

N: What is something that is happening now with the church? Are there any big movements going on?
P: Well, it's been 15 years since it's been painted inside upstairs. We want to get the sanctuary painted. I'm on the properties committee, and we're trying to decide what color. The last time it was painted it was done voluntarily by a contractor whose son had been to Western Carolina and had come to our church for four years. The father was thanking our church by painting the sanctuary, which was really nice. I don't think we're gonna have that again so we'll have to pay for this time. When we can get that all spiffy looking, we're gonna put some new lighting in and some new ceiling fans in the sanctuary that will look a little nicer. That's the materialistic thing. But also what we do as a church mission-wise...we get so many different projects going locally, nationally, and internationally that are really helpful. That is the most important thing we do. Jeffrey and Tonya are really good about bringing our attention to what is needed and what we need to work on.
C: The feeding program with children during the summer has been greatly accepted by the church. We're talking

about some other things to add to that. We haven't gotten to those yet because we want to be sure when we do it that it's something the church supports. That one or two people are not doin' it by themselves.

N: Do you have any stories you'd like to share?
C: This spring, four of us took a mission trip to Arkansas where we'd been involved with a CBF effort there. Their churches were probably not all that much smaller than ours in membership, but they really did need some help. The communities were really destitute. This was in Helena, Arkansas, right on the Mississippi. There was a pastor there who had had a stroke. He had been preaching while recovering and preaching out of his wheelchair. We went in and built a ramp system so he could get up to his pulpit. Then we did some other repairs on that church. We fixed a window that was leaking and did some roof repairs. It took us half a day to do that, but we talked with the pastor afterwards about the sense of being able to get rolled in with the wheelchair and get to that ramp. The sense he had in being able to give that message from the pulpit was pretty strong. Other than that we went to another little community out in the country. I mean it was really out there. It's on a road that dead-ends into a river. And there's a little community that you could see at one time had been a thriving farming community. The houses were pretty poor-quality houses, most of them, and many were vacant. This black church out there had set up a mission of its own there in that little community and they had gotten a mobile classroom from a school that had closed down, a big metal modular–home–type thing. We painted it inside and did some general repairs, but it was just a start for them. We coulda worked on that one building for two or three weeks. I mean there were a lot of things we could've done to it. But the best part of that was they invited us the next Sunday to come to their church. It was just a really welcoming experience to be there. And a very moving experience. The topic that Sunday was their children and youth. It was commemorating some race riots of about 1911, something like that, where hundreds of people were killed, and it was a real meaningful experience. That was them recognizing their own history, beginning to understand their own history, and coming from that point to the time when you have a black president. That's a pretty big swing. They were just real open, and I don't have any doubt that if I'm ever in Helena, Arkansas, I'm welcome in that church. That's a good feeling.

N: What would you like to say to the future readers of the anniversary book?
P: I've always been in a very large church. My dad was a preacher so I was raised in a church. Every church I've belonged to has been large until I came to Cullowhee Baptist. I've learned that you have more responsibilities, more jobs, more things to do because in a small church you still have as much work but fewer people. I know some people complain sometimes, but we get things done. You really have to volunteer a lot more and be aware that if you don't do it, it might not get done. So sometimes the committees are hard, the meetings and all that, everything to go to. But we

usually get things done. I've learned in a smaller church you're responsible to take on more things. And it's still a blessing because things do get done.
C: For the future group, always try and move forward. And remember that's part of the history. This church has always moved forward. It moved here from another place, it moved to a couple locations before it got to where it is now. History is important and I believe in that. I hope that the strong stands this church is making on some issues continues.
P: I hope the church will stay open for all faiths because we have international students at Western. I know that a Hindu student came in. He said he had told his mother that there's not a place for him anywhere nearby. And she said, "Just go into the nearest church." He came in one day and told Jeffrey that and Jeffrey said, "We'll be open for you any time." So he used our church that year he was here, just coming in quietly by himself during the day. So I hope it'll be open for all faiths that need a place anytime.

Interview: Hilary Lindler

Date: July 12, 2011

by Nicole Jarosinski

N: How long have you been secretary?
H: I started in January 2008. I worked there for a year and a half and then quit so I could go to grad school. I'm still in grad school, but they asked me to come back in May 2011.

N: What do you do as secretary?
H: I'm really surprised at how much there is to do. I didn't realize how much goes into keeping a church running. Because you go to church and the bulletins are always there and things are always already figured out when you show up. You don't realize somebody has to decide what songs are gonna be used, and somebody has to pull together the bulletin stuff. It's the same with the newsletter. There's so much that goes into the mundane activities that we never think about. I maintain basic office stuff so the pastors can do their job without having to worry about everything else. They can focus on their pastoral duties.

N: What has been a significant moment for you at the church?
H: I've been in Cullowhee since 2003 when I first came to start my undergraduate degree. I enjoyed the area but I just wandered around because when you live in dormitories you're not really part of the community. You're living in it but you're not of it. And the job has been significant for me because it plopped me into a tight-knit community of people and they do a lot of things together. A lot of people show up for Wednesday night meals and a lot of people are very active with volunteering. I was able to get involved with this already active inclusive community, and it eased the transition from being a college student to being an actual resident in Cullowhee. And it had a lot to do with me being com-

fortable living here and with me falling in love with the area. Now I've got real personal connections. It contributed a sense of interconnectedness and a sense of belonging for me that I needed when I felt like I was floating. Overall it's been a really good experience. Jeffrey and Tonya are great people to work for. They're pleasant and understanding. They helped me get into the groove of things and eased the transition.

N: Is there anything you look forward to every year related to the church?

H: First of all, I always look forward to the Christmas season. It's a lot of work but I love getting ready for the season and the Hanging of the Greens. Christmas in general is one of my favorite religious holidays, and it's cool to be a part of that behind the scenes.

Interview: Laura Stiens

Date: July 19, 2011

by Nicole Jarosinski

N: Laura I know you're in the choir. Can you tell me a little bit about that?

L: I've been in the choir since 1998, and I filled in sometimes when the choir director's not been there. For the big part I enjoy the music. I enjoy singing so it's been a big part of my time there.

N: How did you first choose Cullowhee Baptist Church?

L: We decided the church we were at wasn't a good fit anymore. My parents started looking around and I started looking around and we just ended up there. I went one Sunday and just felt at home and stayed here ever since.

N: What was it that made you feel like home?

L: Just the warm welcome. There were people I knew who I didn't realize went to church here, so they kind of helped welcome me in also.

N: What was a significant moment for you as a member?

L: Probably when Tonya and Jeffrey came, just having the two pastors and the things we went through, how the church all stood together behind Tonya and supported her no matter what, the values that we all had, knowing that it was her calling and like she says "You can't tell God no." That was a big part.

N: I've been trying to piece together that story from as many different people as I can. Can you tell me what you remember about that time?

L: I know we were members with the Tuckaseigee Baptist Association, which is more Southern Baptist. And that was around the time that Southern Baptists did not believe in women being in ministry. I think they were even firing people who believed this. The Association is big Southern Baptist, so they did not want our church being a part because we have a woman pastor. We have women deacons too, so I don't know why there was no issue made about that. But with Tonya coming and being more in the leadership role, there was a lot of controversy. There were four big churches that pulled out when we did too. I never went to any Association meetings or anything, but I know we had meetings at church about where our church stood and what we wanted to do. We fought 'em for a little while and finally just said, "That's enough," and pulled out of the Association.

N: I like how the churches stuck together. There seems to be a culture or a mentality in Baptist churches of "We'll tell ourselves what to do. You're not gonna tell us what to do." They seem to be a lot more autonomous than others.
L: Yeah, there's different groups. There's Southern Baptist, there's CBF that we're a part of, and now we're in with the Western North Carolina Baptist Network. It has churches in Asheville, like First Baptist Asheville, I think First Baptist Sylva's in it, East Sylva, Weaverville, all western parts of the state, that we are associated with now. I don't know who laid the groundwork for that, but it started after we pulled out of the Tuckaseigee Baptist Association.

N: What stands out to you about Cullowhee Baptist Church? What do you think of?
L: It's a welcoming place to be.
N: How have you been affected by the church or its members? How has it impacted your life?
L: Probably just how everybody pulls together. Our house burned in 2009 on the day Aidan was supposed to be born. It was also while I was finishing nursing school; I was taking my final exam. We had an overwhelming amount of support and gifts. I mean Aidan had more stuff after the fire than he did before. And donations monetarily, things for the baby, things for me. We had stuff just show up from the whole community, but the church was a big support, more than I expected to see.

N: What do you look forward to every year in the church?
L: I like the Christmas season because we do more music every week. And Easter too. We do the Palm Sunday service that's so different than any other regular service. It's more music and then we leave in silence. It's just a totally different format. We started it several years ago, and it's become an annual service. It has a lot of meaning. Real powerful. You know how every Sunday we sing *Blest be the Tie,* well that's the one Sunday in the year we do not. The choir sings a song and then everybody leaves in silence. We go through big events leading up to Christ's death so the way the service ends it, Christ has just been crucified, so you leave with that in mind. That's one of the most powerful services I think we do.

N: What has been your happiest moment with the church?
L: Probably Aidan's dedication. We did

that on Christmas Eve, so that was a neat time to do it. It was special for me.

N: Do you have a message, anything you would like to say to future members?
L: Welcome, and I hope they find the church as welcoming and warm and will be able to feel as comfortable as I did. I know it's not the same for everybody, but I hope they feel a part.

N: Do you have any stories you'd like to share?
L: Well, my son can sometimes be competition for Steve. If we don't have childcare for Aidan, he'll try to imitate Steve directing. Of course then everybody especially the younger ones, kinda get distracted. So then Steve's like "Okay now, I'm the director. He's not the director yet." Steve takes it all in stride, you know. But then sometimes he'll make sure we have childcare too (laughs). But Aidan does pretty good though. They say he's the future director.

Interview: Amanda Smith

Date: June 28, 2011

by Nicole Jarosinski

N: I'm speaking with Amanda Smith, who is going to share her experiences from Cullowhee Baptist Church. First question, you are the college intern right?
A: I was last summer. I'm a student here at Western. I'll be a senior in the fall.

N: I see you in the office all the time, are you helping out?
A: I volunteered in the office last school year. I'm just spending a few weeks here this summer just to help out. That's why I'm always here.

N: Just so I know, you're not a member.
A: I'm not. I just come here in the school year and when I'm here in the summer.

N: It's your home-away-from-home church.
A: Exactly.

N: Why did you choose Cullowhee Baptist? Why did you first come here?
A: My freshman year I lived up on the hill in Reynolds. The church is right here at the foot of the hill from the dorm. My roommate was Baptist as well, so we started talking about trying to find a church. We thought we'd start at going to Cullowhee Baptist, but our plan was to go around to different churches in the community. We started here, though, because it was convenient. Then a couple weeks into it, my roommate got invited to work with the children and she asked if I wanted to go along and I said sure. Steve Baxley asked us to start working with the kids and about a month later he said, "Fill out these forms and it'll be a job and we'll pay you." So we got the job to work with the kids. Christine and I thought, "This is God saying we should stay here and not

look for another church." So since then, Christine and I have both been coming.

N: What drew you when you were visting?
A: It's a lot like my home church. It's a small congregation. Everybody knows everybody. There are a lot of community people. And the numbers are the same. It's almost exactly like being back home, which is really cool. Tonya and Jeffrey, the pastors, they're great. Everybody was so welcoming. And your first Sunday back on campus, everybody's going to be more welcoming. But it wasn't just like they welcomed us the first couple weeks of the year and then forgot about us. They try to involve the college students while they're here, and that meant a lot, just knowing they wanted us here.

N: How do you feel you've been accepted by the people? Could you elaborate?
A: My sophomore year, the fall of 2009, we gained an associate pastor for two years. So the church started being more active with the college ministry. We did a lot of activities on the weeknights, then Sunday after church we'd go eat together. So the college ministry, with our associate pastor Richard Goddard, was what really helped to be accepted even more than I was already. This past year they invited me to be on the college ministry committee. They're pulling me in some more now.

N: When you think about your time here in Cullowhee Baptist, what do you remember the most?
A: Last summer as the intern and getting involved with all the different ministries. Being out in the community and helping people, I think, is a big part of what Cullowhee Baptist is doing to share God's love with everybody. Especially the summer feeding ministry they started last year. I got to help jumpstart and direct all the volunteers and things. That was definitely something I remember, which is why I'm here this week again working with the program.

N: How have you been affected by Cullowhee Baptist? How has it impacted your life?
A: Well, freshman year I was just here on Sundays and Wednesdays. We worked with the kids on Wednesdays and then of course worship on Sunday. But once the college ministry started sophomore year, I started becoming more involved and the church started impacting me. I had somewhere to go and I had a place where I felt totally accepted. I spend time with not only people my age but other members of the church as well. We had a game night and some of the people from the college committee would come and hang out with us. Having that family away from home, they really opened up and treated me like one of their own even though I'm not originally from here and haven't been here long.

N: Tell me about the time you've been here. Maybe about the summer feeding program?
A: Last summer with the program I was involved in everything. I ran a site up in Little Canada community, which just amazes me how far away they are. You turn at the river in Tuckasegee, go another ten miles up the mountain. They're way up there. Those kids don't get to come down the mountain a lot. Going to Sylva is a big deal for them. I

had no idea it was even there until last summer. The one family that we mainly fed ended up moving closer to Tuckasegee Baptist, so we had fewer and fewer members at Little Canada. Eventually we had to stop that site, but we still deliver Manna packs to families on Fridays. It's a five pound bag of groceries, so they have groceries for about a week. We're doing it there and for Wayehutta community. We still help at the River Park Trailer Park. One of our youth lives there, so it's a big deal to have our presence there as well.

N: Can you tell me about some of the kids who live there?
A: Last summer there was a lot of violence in the trailer park and there are so many kids that live there. And like I said, one of our youth lives there. Knowing all that goes on and having all those kids living there, I mean it's hard for anybody to live there, but especially the kids. Getting in the trailer park and letting those kids know that someone does care about them, even with all the bad, crazy stuff going on, I think was really important for us. This year things haven't been quite as crazy with the police involvement, but there are a lot of kids down there that we're not reaching, that we didn't reach last summer because the parents were afraid to let the kids outside. One day I went down there with Jeffrey and we had a few extra meals. Technically we're supposed to keep those, but Jeffrey knew a family that came regularly but wasn't there that day. We drove up to their trailer and they were there, but they had been afraid to let the kids come out. So we stopped and gave them a couple of extra lunches. Technically we weren't supposed to, but Jeffrey said, "I'm feeding these kids. It doesn't matter about the rules. We're going to feed these children." That was really cool. Jeffrey's passionate about this program. I think his enthusiasm is contagious. I hope that people who are working for the program this summer get as much out of it as I did last summer. It's been a blessing to work with all those kids.

The really cool thing was the Presbyterian Church in Sylva and another church have picked up three sites in Sylva. It was really cool to see our work expand across the community and how other people want to get in it. It's really cool that we could do this for free. Because Jackson County's free and reduced lunch rate [for students during the school year] is over 50%, we don't have to ask for anything to make sure each child gets free or reduced lunch. Everybody gets to partake regardless, which is really cool too.

N: This church really does take care of their own.
A: Yeah, that's another thing that drove me to this church. I love missions in general. If you feel called to go overseas that's fine, but I'm really passionate about local stuff just because I think we have to help ourselves first before we can help other people. So I thought it was really cool that they look after their community that much. Not just the people who go to this church, but the people who don't go to this church too.

N: What do you look forward to every year here at the church?
A: It sounds kinda cheesy but I really do

look forward to every Sunday. There's the whole experience itself, but I really enjoy after everything's over we sing "Blest Be the Tie" and go out for the week. But then I love Wednesday nights. It's one of my favorite things.

N: What happens Wednesday night?
A: On Wednesday nights everybody gets together at 5:30 and has a meal, which is free for college students, so that makes us very happy. They know we don't have the money to pay for a meal, and we can get a home-cooked meal instead of having to eat in the dining hall. Even for families it's pretty inexpensive. Sometimes it's home-cooked, sometimes it's catered from a restaurant. Everybody gets together for the meal and hangs out. College students are there, our 80-year-old members are there. Cullowhee is really big about sharing meals with people and fellowshiping. At 6:00 they have an adult Bible study in the fellowship hall. Sometimes they have speakers come in. We've had a few missionaries, some who are from North Carolina. It's always really cool when they bring in speakers because the kids and youth are learning about the missionaries in their classrooms. They get to see the people they're learning about. The kids do their own little thing. It's called M & Ms—Music and Missions. We'll do a mission story with them, do a craft or a game from the country we're studying about, then go upstairs and practice the music they'll sing on Sunday. So that was really cool for me to get to do.

Last summer I started working with the youth, which was a good idea because our youth right now is all middle school girls and one guy. Richard mainly led the youth, but they wanted a girl up there too so we could have both. Every Wednesday night he taught and I helped, but since he left in May, I'm gonna teach the youth in the fall with Matt Brown, the chairman of the deacons. I'm really excited about that. I want to teach when I graduate, so I get to practice those sorts of things now. The kids are doing Heifer International, so we've had luncheons to help raise money for them. They're trying to raise $5,000 to buy an ark of animals and send it to a country. They've been working on it for a couple of years, and they're halfway there. For five or six kids to raise that much money so far, it's really exciting.

N: As a younger attendee and a woman, how do you feel about having co-pastors?
A: I love the co-pastor, husband-and-wife pastor team. That was new to me when I got here. I had never even heard of Cooperative Baptist Fellowship or women being a pastor in a Baptist church. It's pretty inspiring really, especially to see Tonya and the struggles she's had to overcome being a female pastor. It's been really cool to get to know her, her story, and where she's come from. I have thought about going into ministry, so it's good to know there is a group that accepts women. My thought is God made all of us; I don't think he cares whether I'm a man or a woman as long as I'm preaching his word the correct way. That's what my grandma said when she found out. "Well as long as she's preaching from the Bible." And that's my interpretation. It's really sad for the people who can't accept

that because Tonya's a great preacher. You can tell she preaches from the heart.

N: What has been a significant moment for you as someone who goes to this church?

A: Seeing the college ministry grow. I've heard from some members that this past year had the most college students consistently in worship. Usually we'd have 20 at least. Used to be that many may come the first couple Sundays, but then it'd dwindle down to just 10. Ten is still good of course, but being right here on campus, you'd think there'd be more. This past year was our first year as an official student organization here on campus. We're called the Cooperative Student Fellowship. We're sponsored by the CBF, so we have people from different denominations as well. We'll meet on Monday nights and do a Bible study. We do a lot of mission stuff. Sometimes we'll partner with the church and do things too.

N: Can you tell me any stories about the university outreach?

A: Like I said, we do a lot of mission stuff. Richard, our associate pastor for the past two years, was a college minister as well. And Steve Baxley, the minister of music here, is our faculty advisor because he works at Western. The year before we were official, we took our first mission trip together. We went to Miami to help Touching Miami with Love. There were six of us and Richard. We were down for a week to [work in] a day camp cuz the kids had spring break the same week we did. The kids were there pretty much all day. The camp was in Overtown, a community outside Miami, and it's one of the poorest communities of Miami. As you can imagine, those kids have pretty rough home lives. My favorite part of the mission trip was taking them to a museum. It was an hour ride, so kids had a lot of fun on the bus. And when we got there, some of the kids had never seen an escalator. They had the most fun running up and down. Some were more calm and just rode it up and down. Of course, some people were angry about that, but I thought, just let them have fun. They're not hurting anybody. The joy those kids had. That mission trip and a lot of stuff the college ministry has done reminds me of the things we take for granted.

N: The church seems to bring together the university and the community. It's a meeting ground.

A: It's been really cool to see how they try to bridge things together between the two, the real Cullowhee and the university. A lot of people say "Oh, Cullowhee's just Western Carolina." But there's a whole community of people who have been here their entire lives and for generations. Going to this church has helped me to see that. So when Western started talking about expansion, I thought, well I'm sure no one's bothered to ask the real people of Cullowhee or Forest Hills. So for my political science class we tried to do a survey of the people of Forest Hills to find out what they thought about annexing. That came out of being here at Cullowhee Baptist and knowing people who live in the community, who don't necessarily agree with what the big people on campus want to do.

N: I'm not saying Cullowhee couldn't use

some spiffing up.
A: Oh yeah. I mean, I came to Western because it was small. I don' t personally want the big shopping center kind of stuff. I'm from a small town, so if I wanted a big school, I would have gone somewhere else. I'm not for all of that. Yes, it does need something done, especially the Old Cullowhee part.

N: Yeah, three closed gas stations are not pretty.
A: Exactly. So there's work to be done, but we don't have to go all out. Of course the shopping center they're wanting to build on campus is not really back here. I think the community would benefit if they expanded back here on Old Cullowhee [Road]. I think the college students and the community could both benefit from that. I'm sure if they put something inside campus, a lot of the community isn't gonna go to that.

N: No, I don't think I've ever seen any locals at McAlister's Deli on campus, even though it's the best restaurant for miles. Plus you can't park anywhere before 5pm.
A: Exactly. The library staff at Western uses part of our parking lot here at the church. We're lucky we have the parking we do, I guess.

N: It's a shame because the church was here first.
A: Exactly. Exactly.

N: What other obstacles has the church or the people overcome since you've been here?
A: I think getting people in the community and on campus to come to church. We talked a lot about community outreach. Part of that is to help other people. But I think part of it too is to get our name out there so people will be interested. I think we've done a really good job of that. I've seen new families come into the church since I've been here. We've added a couple youth and their families. Of course there's so many little Baptist churches in this area that it's kinda hard.

N: What was your happiest moment in your time at Cullowhee Baptist?
A: Last year when they asked me to be the intern. Wanda Kidd runs the intern program. What usually happens is the church applies for an intern and you apply for an internship, then Wanda will place you somewhere. Having the church ask me to be their intern instead of getting stuck somewhere random, that was the point where I felt like a was actually a part of the church. I kind of already did because of working with the children Wednesday nights, but getting asked to do the internship said to me, "We want you to learn more about our church, we want you to be a part of it and not just another college student." So that was really exciting for me to do and getting to know everybody. Before that I didn't know names or I would know names but not faces. And they still talk to me even though I'm not the intern anymore. They still want me to do things with the church and go eat with them.

N: Tell me about the associate pastor Richard.
A: He's from Florida; he did his undergrad at Samford in Alabama, then did his seminary at Baylor and applied to be a

minister-in-residence through the Cooperate Baptist Fellowship. He got here in June of '09. His official title was associate pastor, but basically he was the associate pastor, the secretary, the college minster, the children and youth minister, and pretty much whatever else needed doing. I got to know him first through the college ministry and then with youth. He led our Bible study for college ministry on Monday nights. He went with us on our mission project. Pretty much anything the college kids were doing, he was there. He also contributed to the college student population because every Sunday morning he wouldn't just go and sit down. He'd be talking to people throughout the congregation, usually the college students first. He would remember your name, he would remember stuff about you. People felt like he cared about them, which he did. And he was my boss for working with the kids. Before I started the food program, most of the stuff I did was to help Richard out. Every Wednesday night I was with him working with the youth. He was really good at making connections with college students and then including them in on things. Then this past year when we started our student organization, I was the president and I had to work with him a lot. But then he left. His program was only for two years. So he finished up in May and I came back for his last Sunday. Seeing all the contributions he made to the church in two years and then leaving. I don't do well with goodbyes or change, but I had them both together. It was sad to see him leave. But I'm really excited about what he has to do in the future, and we're getting a new minister.

Rear-Matthew Brown
Richard Goddard

N: Can you tell me any stories about him?

A: He was very funny. Oh goodness. So many stories. I know on his last Sunday the chairman of deacons was giving him a gift and listing the things he was going to miss about Richard. One of them was that Richard paces when he gets nervous or doesn't have things planned out. So Matt said, "I always knew when he had to teach or do something, that he would pace back and forth." One of the last Sundays he was here we had a worship service at the nursing home, because they'll go and do services every other month or so at one of the nursing homes in Sylva. Matt had seen him pacing, and I had too, but I knew that Richard was supposed to speak. Matt walked over to him and asked, "Are you preaching today?" Yeah he was, and Matt said, "I could tell cuz you were pacing back and forth." He'd do that with the youth and college students if he didn't know exactly what was going on.

And then he can't stand when he doesn't know when a conversation's gonna end. If it's just gonna keep going and going and going. On our mission trip to Alabama over spring break, we had just got done painting the window sills inside the church. We came outside and were cleaning our brushes and an elderly man stopped by. He was a member of the church who wanted to stop by and thank us for what we were doing. So here all of us sit down on the steps and at first Richard is standing talking to him thinking he's only gonna talk for a few minutes. Well, 30 minutes went by and you could tell Richard's thinking this is not gonna end. He finally sits down on the steps. We found out through the conversation that the man had been mayor of the town for 12 years and had taught school for at least 35 years. So he had lots of stories to tell. He talked for like an hour. It was really funny to watch Richard's reaction to this because he doesn't do well with long conversations or long meetings. Our leadership team meetings would always last a really long time and he didn't like that at all. But it was really funny after the fact.

And he was a big Florida Gators fan. A lot of the people who go to this church are Georgia fans, so football season was always fun to watch. They would make comments to each other in passing. Sometimes something would come from the pulpit when a deacon was speaking. He'd end by saying, "Go Gators!" Richard has stuffed animals from all the colleges he's been to, so last summer he had his Florida Gator sitting in the office on the second floor. And Jim Dean, pastor of the Summit Church who has his office here on the third floor, decided to kidnap Richard's alligator and take him along on a trip. So Jim Dean kidnapped it, named him Albert, made him a Facebook page, and started posting pictures of where Albert had been. Then the college students decided we wanted to do the same thing. Some of our members are band students and they went to Pasadena for the Rose Bowl Parade with the marching band. They kidnapped Albert, took him with them, and posted pictures on Facebook. Melani, one of our college students, decided to tag Richard on all these pictures. At the time he was getting Facebook notifications on his phone, and he said, "After 60 I disabled that," because she tagged him in 100 pictures. Then I kidnapped Albert and took him with me to New York for a conference. Of course we stuck him in the snow because it was snowing up there. Richard hates the snow. It was great. Who knew you could have that much fun with a grown man's stuffed animal?!

N: Is there anything you would like to say to future members or college visitors?
A: For college students, even though Cullowhee is really good about making sure you get involved, you have to want to get involved yourself. So when the pastors say on Sunday, "We're doing this mission opportunity. We need volunteers," I think you have to be willing to ask them if you can help. Especially with our generation a lot of people want others to come to them, but everybody in the church is so busy doing so many things. They can't always come to you every single time they need help. Volunteering in the church office, they didn't ask me to do that. I asked them. So my advice is, you have to get yourself involved. And my advice to future church members is make the college students feel welcome so they'll want to stay. I think it's a two-way street.

Some History of

The Membership of Cullowhee Baptist Church

by Etheree Chancellor and Dianne Yount

Master Membership List

November 21, 1821–present

When I retired after more than 18 years as church secretary, I planned to make a master membership list of Cullowhee Baptist Church. Finally, several months ago, I started the project. I would like to thank those who have assisted me: Barbara Dooley, Pam Hill, Mary Lou Millwood, and Tonya Vickery.

From the minutes we saw that those Christians were imperfect people as we Christians are today. We read that their struggles to stay true to their faith is in many cases, the same as ours. The research has been sad, funny, unbelievable, and rewarding. The list has been compiled using the best information we could determine from the records. Many pages were illegible because of age; some had been removed from the book altogether; and for some, the handwriting was virtually illegible. Many names were spelled as the person recording the information heard them, making it even more difficult to know exactly who was who. Because of the length of the membership list (over 4,000 names), the church has placed the list in its entirety on our website: **www.cullowheebaptist.com**.

When viewing the list, you will note that we have put many names in parentheses; this is to indicate there are questions of exactly which spelling is correct or if the person listed could be the same as another name listed as an initial or initials.

In the fourth column, the dates listed indicate whether the person joined by baptism or letter. To try to list whether a person joined "by experience," "on profession of faith," "by baptism," or "by letter" would have been difficult to do organizationally. Some were listed on one page as joining by one way, and on another page they might be listed as having joined a different way on a different date. Because of this, we listed those who joined "by experience," "profession of faith," and "baptism" as having joined by "baptism."

In the fifth column, you will notice that some members were dismissed the same day they joined. That information is correct. Also, some names listed indicate persons joining, leaving, and then coming back into the Cullowhee Baptist membership.

We realize there is information not found in this list that can be found in the Cullowhee Baptist Cemetery. The intent of this list, however, was to record exactly, to the best of our ability, the names of members and how they are listed in the minutes covering 190 years of Cullowhee Baptist history.

You may find several names that seem to be duplicates—and they may indeed be duplicates. If we were not 100 percent certain one person was the same as another on the list, we included the names twice (or perhaps even more times!) so we could be sure no one was left off the list. So as you look at the list, may you enjoy finding names and remembering when....